Strength Through Weakness

GREG BECKER

WESTBOW
PRESS®
A DIVISION OF THOMAS NELSON
& ZONDERVAN

WestBow Press books may be ordered through booksellers or by contacting:

WestBow Press
A Division of Thomas Nelson & Zondervan
1663 Liberty Drive
Bloomington, IN 47403
www.westbowpress.com
1 (866) 928-1240

ISBN: 978-1-9736-3064-7 (sc)
ISBN: 978-1-9736-3063-0 (hc)
ISBN: 978-1-9736-3065-4 (e)

Library of Congress Control Number: 2018907094

Print information available on the last page.

WestBow Press rev. date: 08/09/2018

But he said to me, "My grace is sufficient for you, for my power is made perfect in weakness." Therefore I will boast all the more gladly about my weaknesses, so that Christ's power may rest on me. That is why, for Christ's sake, I delight in weaknesses, in insults, in hardships, in persecutions, in difficulties. For when I am weak, then I am strong.

2 Corinthians 12:9-10

"I am so convicted by this unction of the Holy Spirit that I am running as if in the closing meters of the race that has been coursed by His creative and wise plan. The pain and exhilaration is a thrill to be asked to perform in. The Lord has allowed me to flourish in team competition for 55 years. This may be my final chance to be used for a victorious cause by His winning hand."

—An email from Greg as he was finishing his book a month before he died.

"The hand of The Master Planner has unquestionably authored this story of strength through weakness. His grace has indeed been sufficient. You see, this is not my story personally. This is the story of a caring God that never fails to faithfully see us through life's every battle and blessing. He provides beyond all that we could ask or imagine. His is the strong and sure yoke that is easy for those of us that labor in the midst of heavy burdens. He has promised an abundant life when we invite Him into our lives. I trust you have seen the hand of God in this letter and not the weak and frail hand of this author."

—Greg Becker

Contents

Dedication

This book is dedicated to my sweetheart for life, Debra L. (Spencer) Becker. I first met Debbie in the seventh grade at John R. Lea Intermediate School, which is a part of the Southeast Local School District in rural and family farm dominated Wayne County, Ohio. In the mid 1950's, four small villages and their respective communities consolidated into a school district that brought the little communities together. The high school in this district is known as Waynedale. The school mascot and athletic teams are called the Golden Bears.

I only knew Debbie from afar for the first few years. Never in my wildest imagination did I imagine this bright, beautiful, and popular girl would show much interest in an immature underachiever, such as myself. My faith in Christ led her to show enough interest in me that to my great and blessed surprise she agreed to go out on our first date. Our date followed the Friday night Golden Bear football game, in which I played, in October of 1973.

That date began a relationship that has flourished in love and endurance through a truly wild ride of ups and downs while living in the midst of the good and not so good things of life. I am so grateful that Debbie has been my rock of consistent love and support, especially while battling cancer and the subsequent medical challenges that spun out of that dreaded disease over the past 34 years.

We were united in marriage on October 7th, 1978. It was a beautiful, sunshine-filled fall afternoon at the little Church of Christ in the village of Fredericksburg, Ohio. Debbie brought light into the darkness of the cancer and medical trials I endured, especially by birthing our daughters, Katelyn and Kelsey. Deb nurtured and molded our daughters into the strong, responsible young women of faith they are today.

To this day, she continues to use her gifts of intellect, kindness, competence, faith, strength, and compassion to bring joy into my life, our family, and that of others that she has touched. Throughout this memoir, you will sense that the hand of God and a dedicated Christian wife are the constants throughout the journey.

It is with my love and respect that I dedicate this book to Debbie. It is my prayer that she will be honored and blessed as a result of the spiritual fruit I desire for this book.

Acknowledgements

It is through the mighty arm of the Lord that these acknowledgments can be expressed. I claim Jesus Christ as my personal Savior that has moved in miraculous ways to use the life of this child of God to bring Him a bit of the glory that He deserves. I acknowledge that all righteousness that we can know and experience is through His Spirit, which provides abundance in this life and the life to come.

The title for this book, "Strength Through Weakness," comes from a Bible passage penned by the Apostle Paul who has been a guiding example of flourishing in life in spite of a "thorn in the flesh." While writing to the people of Corinth, he explains that three times he prayed to God to remove the "thorn in the flesh," which we would acknowledge as a disease or distress. God did not grant Paul's petition. However, Paul would come to the realization that this thorn was actually a gift that drew him nearer to God. Paul states he learned that God's grace is sufficient. And so he was given a "thorn in the flesh," in order that He might gain strength through weakness.

The list of men, women, relatives, friends, and medical professionals is far too extensive to acknowledge in this short synopsis. It is with deep appreciation that I acknowledge the contributions each individual has made, as our paths have intersected while living in the midst of them.

First and foremost, I acknowledge the profound love and support of my wife, daughters, and new son-in-law, Debbie, Katelyn, Kelsey, and Nate. Each of you continue to bring joy, love, and hope to my life. I am so thankful and filled with pride, because of the Christian love that is the core of your respective hearts.

I honor the tremendous legacy that my parents, Larry and Eloise, provided as they nurtured and molded me. They provided a firm foundation that has contributed to any resolve, strength, or goodness I have been privileged to demonstrate in this life. I also acknowledge my siblings Gerry, Doug, and Jennifer. Equally, I recognize my Uncle Jack and Aunt Elaine Robinson and their adult children Mick, Kathy, Lynne, Tod, and Sally.

The people of faith that are to be acknowledged are beyond my ability to list here. However, two men that have served as spiritual mentors deserve special acknowledgement. They are Pastor Henry Hudson and his dear lifetime Christian friend and highly accomplished businessman, Norman Gidney. These genuine men of God have been an encouragement throughout my life and particularly in regard to my move into full-time ministry and the writing of this book.

My dear friends combine to serve as an influence that has brought happiness, support, and inspiration as together we have traversed the ups and downs of life. It is an impossible task to know where to begin in listing these precious friends. Allow me to say that each of you are held close in my heart and I will continue to give you thanks for all you have done in my behalf.

Many medical professionals have been at the forefront of my physical survival. Special thanks are extended to Dan Queener, MD; and my friend, neighbor, and cardiologist, Dr. George "Skip" Seese.

I am truly a man abounding in the blessings of these and other wonderful people that have guided and directed me throughout. "Strength Through Weakness," is my acknowledgement of the power of Christ and the people that have been moved to provide salt and light in this life. May each person sense the grace of God in their respective lives.

Preface - A Personal Narrative and Principles for Application

This is a book that uses my personal narrative to give you, the reader, a sense of what it is like to go through cancer and other life threatening diseases. Together, we will see how it is true that the weaker I get, the stronger I become. Along with my life story, specific Bible passages that reference principled living are provided for living in the midst of challenges that appear on our respective paths through life. Another objective of the book is to provide an opportunity to personally reflect on where we are in living out these principles. Pictures, for perspective, are also included to give you a glimpse of the people and places about which I have written. As work on this manuscript has taken on life, it has been my thought that when we have no dream, we have no destiny. My dream is that this book will influence your destiny, which is yet to be determined.

Introduction

It is a land the LORD your God cares for; the eyes of the LORD your God are continually on it from the beginning of the year to its end. Deuteronomy 11:12 (NIV)

First and foremost I want to sincerely thank you for picking up this book. It is my heart-felt prayer that the words will inspire you to gain strength even as your body may weaken while living in the midst of disease and distress.

It was a life-altering, cloudy November day in 1978 in the heart of the rust belt of the Midwest United States. Dr. Dan Queener had just entered my hospital room and was informing me, as a 21 year old newlywed, that during his surgical procedure on me, he had removed a malignant tumor. We were at Dunlap Community Hospital in the small town of Orrville, Ohio, where life was comfortable and slow paced. This was a safe and protected area in which to grow up. Yet, I was being informed of unparalleled danger. I had an aggressive, deadly cancer that, untreated, would kill me in a matter of months.

This was a stunning revelation to a strong, fit, athletic young man. It was surreal to be hearing the news of this unimaginable turn of events. Yet, the reality of that day was devastatingly true; this was not a bad dream from which I could awaken. Young Dr.

Dan Queener, who had just set up his private medical practice in nearby Massillon, Ohio, presented the news compassionately, yet professionally.

Dan did not linger in emotional blather. He confidently presented his plan of attack to eradicate and defeat the deadly disease. The treatment would take place five hours away at Indiana University Medical Center in Indianapolis, Indiana. There at IUMC a brilliant team of physician cancer research specialists had developed a cutting edge chemotherapy protocol, specifically for my kind of cancer, under the leadership of Dr. Lawrence Einhorn. Years later, the same physician team and medical protocol would save the life of Lance Armstrong. Armstrong is known internationally as an Olympic gold medalist and multiple Tour de' France bicycle racing champion.

When the news of the diagnosis and subsequent course of treatment had been explained, I found myself in solitude in the hospital room in unfamiliar surroundings. My mind raced with questions, puzzlement, anger, and fear. How could this be happening to me? I had not abused my body. My life was just beginning as planned. I had a new, beautiful wife that I was prepared to flourish with in life. I had a career to build; an exciting, adventurous life to live. Everything had fallen into place, as I was sure that God had blessed and prospered me because of my love for Him.

It was impossible to imagine defeat would come from this disease. My athletic achievements had established that I was a consistent winner on winning teams. I was a winner, not a loser. Cancer victims lost, and I would not allow my mind to imagine this would be my fate. So, I entered my battle with great resolve and the cockiness of youth, because I was strong in body, mind, and soul. My initial reliance would be on my personal, physical strength. The God of this universe would reveal to me through the forthcoming battles of disease and distress that only through Jesus Christ can a person maintain the resolve and perseverance that exceeds our wildest expectation. Jesus Christ brings strength through weakness in the midst of cancer, and any chronic, catastrophic illness. Out of this foundational relationship, I learned that the most valuable strength is multiplied through personal relationships with people that live in and through Jesus Christ.

As the mysteries of God would have it, this battle with cancer would be the mere tip of the iceberg in my challenges with disease and distress. In the years to come, God would present in my path of life: heart failure, respiratory failure, and the onset of kidney failure after open-heart surgery that was complicated by what the doctors call a bleed out. I will be forever grateful to my thoracic surgeon, Dr. Antonio Chryssos. He worked tirelessly to resolve the bleed out over a nearly 24 hour period of time. The initial surgery took five to six hours. However, just a few hours later it was necessary to take me back into surgery after the initial open heart surgery. Dr. Chryssos would operate a second time to try to stop the bleeding. A few hours after this second surgery, Dr. Chryssos determined that he would need to operate a third time in an effort to stop the profuse bleeding. My life was unquestionably in the balance.

Subsequently, the medical trauma of the lengthy and difficult open heart surgery shut down all kidney function and I began dialysis, which I continue to this day. Each night requires hooking up to my in-home peritoneal dialysis machine next to our bed for eleven hours of treatment. It really isn't as difficult as it might sound. Peritoneal dialysis has been quite easy on my system, and it is wonderful to have the treatments at home, while in our comfortable bed.

Lastly, it has been determined by both the Cleveland Clinic and the Ohio State Medical Center that my physical status qualifies me for a heart/kidney transplant. However, due to poor lung function in combination with my other major organ failures, their respective medical boards of review have determined that they will not proceed with transplantation because of the poor chance for my survival.

The following pages contain what is hoped to be an easy to read overview of my personal biography. I sincerely hope that you, my reader, will be captured by the mystical guidance throughout the life journey that I have traveled. It is my experience that many lives are lived in what could be described as a rather robotic existence. But some, even in the face of catastrophic challenges, break out of the "normal" mold and find Life with a capital L. My reader, the following is how this has been accomplished in my life and how the same can be true for yours.

One of the men that has had a tremendous impact throughout the centuries is the Apostle Paul. He wrote much of the New Testament Scriptures. Paul recalls a "thorn in the flesh." The Bible translation that follows calls it a "handicap." Paul describes this un-revealed disease/distress as a "gift." After unsuccessfully pleading with God to heal him from his disease/distress, Paul comes to the realization that the grace of God is enough to live in the midst of it all. In fact, by this strength through grace, Paul finds good cheer and the perseverance necessary to live a full and productive life, especially for the Lord.

Paul writes: "*Because of the extravagance of those (God's) revelations, and so I wouldn't get a big head, I was given the gift of a handicap (thorn in the flesh) to keep me in constant touch with my limitations. Satan's angel did his best to get me down; what he in fact did was push me to my knees. No danger then of walking around high and mighty!*

At first I didn't think of it as a gift, and begged God to remove it. Three times I did that, and then he told me,

My grace is enough; it's all you need. My strength comes into its own in your weakness. Once I heard that, I was glad to let it happen. I quit focusing on the handicap and began appreciating the gift. It was a case of Christ's strength moving in on my weakness. Now I take limitations in stride, and with good cheer, these limitations that cut me down to size—abuse, accidents, opposition, bad breaks. I just let Christ take over! And so the weaker I get, the stronger I become." 2 Corinthians 12:7-10(MSG).

This is a truly remarkable and powerful word picture of the anxiety Paul was suffering. After unsuccessfully seeking the Lord for healing, a great truth was revealed by God to Paul, which to any normal person is beyond understanding, and that is that God's grace is more than adequate for the most extreme events. Amazingly, although Paul was a remarkably strong man, he learned that his strength was only made perfect in his weakness, which is a completely foreign concept.

Like all supernatural events, it is intellectually unimaginable and impossible to understand what you have never experienced. The challenge this verse creates is to understand how to communicate what is undeniably real but, nevertheless, incomprehensible.

It has been family, friends, and faith that have been the constants throughout the ups and downs of life. Our daughters are the delight of our lives. Katelyn is now married to an outstanding Christian young man by the name of Nathan Shultz. Kelsey is at Malone University during the writing of this book studying to be a special education teacher. I am now blessed to have been married to Debbie for 34 years and have lived 55 years. By the grace of God, I look forward to many more years before the Lord calls me home to heaven.

I am so thankful to say that I continue to live a productive life allowing the Lord to use these life experiences to encourage and comfort others. I trust and pray that you will benefit from reading this first effort by the author at writing a book.

And so begins this journey in print to capture the vital cause and power of Jesus Christ who provides perseverance beyond human reach. "Strength Through Weakness" is my first-hand experience of surviving and thriving, while being consumed by chronic disease and distress. The outline has been formed, the experiences lived, and the fruit is for Jesus Christ.

Chapter 1
Before We Began

Jesus answered, "I am the way and the truth and the life. No one comes to the Father except through me." John 14:6(CEB)

A childhood is a precious and fragile thing that must be protected by those of us privileged to be their caretakers. Telling kids of adult details robs these vulnerable souls of their innocence. Childhood is a one-time proposition. Let your children be children. There will be time for them to be adults. Spare them the full exposure of life, not because you are cheating them; rather, you are guarding their precious hearts and souls. It has been my observation and life experience as a child and a dad that exposing a child to the full spectrum of life is unfair and typically damaging to the future of the child.

Living Carefree

I think back joyfully at the early, carefree days of my childhood in the 60's and early 70's growing up in the small village of Apple Creek, Ohio. I thoroughly enjoyed my childhood. We were blessed with Christian parents that lived a traditional lifestyle in the 1960's. We were raised in a two story Victorian home on Main

Street. It was like living in Mayberry from the 1960's television situation comedy show starring Andy Griffith.

Our parents were strong people of faith that truly loved one another. I was heavily influenced by the example they lived out in front of their boys. My parents joined with a few other families to establish a church known as Calvary Chapel in Massillon, Ohio. The ministry has existed for almost fifty years. I have flourished spiritually, because of my lifetime of experience with the people of Calvary Chapel and their Christian acquaintances.

Dad wore a suit Monday through Saturday to his job as a buyer/department store manager in the county's largest and longest running retail department store. Mom was a stay-at-home mother who cared for my older brother, younger brother and I. My sister, Jennifer, was born ten years after my arrival, breaking the string of boys with whom my patient mother would endure.

Our Mom was, and is, such a nurturing, loving Christian lady. She was very active in various civic clubs, our school, and our church. Mom was the perfect complement to Dad. Together, they were a tremendous couple and set a wonderful example for me and my siblings. I considered my parents as perfect in every way when I was a child, and this perspective is the way it should be in our childhood. As we mature into adults, we should come to realize that our revered parents, like all of us, aren't quite perfect. It is my experience that coming to this realization is imperative to a healthy adult relationship.

Mom was always there for me, especially in the midst of my illnesses and hospital stays. She was fully and intimately engaged, while dad was quietly worrying in the background.

In our younger days, Mom would often lead her easily distracted boys in singing church choruses while traveling in the car. These songs were comprised of lyrics that spelled out practical biblical truths. At home, she would always have the big radio stereo system in the dining room tuned to her favorite radio station, WDBN "The Quiet Island." In a house full of active boys, she was doing everything she could to proactively minimize loud and rambunctious behavior.

Dad brought music into our lives as well. When Dad was home, he would regale us with his trumpet playing expertise, knowledge of the various instruments of the big band music he loved, and singing in the church choir. It was as he sang in the church choir that I would be most embarrassed. He swayed and over-enunciated every word. Wouldn't you know it, our daughter Kelsey, his granddaughter, sings the same way… from the very core of the heart and soul. Oh, how I would treasure just one more opportunity to sing in the church choir with Dad.

Because of his department store management responsibilities, Dad spent a significant part of his day at work. It made me proud to know he was in a position of responsibility with a revered local employer. This view was further validated by the dark suits and ties that served as his work attire. He was widely known throughout the community because of his highly visible job with Freedlander's Department Store.

Mr. Herman Freedlander served as a sort of surrogate father and revered mentor to Dad. Herman was renowned throughout the community for his wonderful spirit, wise business dealings, and generosity. Dad would say two Jews were integral in his life, Jesus Christ and Herman Freedlander.

Meanwhile, Grandpa Howard Becker was a free-spirited, some would say selfish, adventurer who was more interested in being a cowboy out west rather than the husband and dad that he was called to be back home in Apple Creek, Ohio. Dad was just about to enter his formative childhood years when Grandpa left Grandma and him for Colorado. Grandma and Dad would have to fend for themselves in an upstairs apartment above the village pharmacy.

I view this as a truly terrible failure of a father's primary responsibility to be personally engaged with the family God provides. Grandpa's decision to leave his young and yet-to-be established family to pursue his personal dreams caused a lifetime of deleterious consequences for his wife and even more so his son, my dad, Larry Becker.

Nonetheless, upon Grandpa Becker's return to Apple Creek he remained married to Grandma and performed many gestures of kindness for people that came into his life. He was particularly well known for his apple butter making, which was very popular throughout the community. He would cook up the ingredients that made for a rich and tasty spread on bread. He grandiosely prepared this delicious treat in two huge brass kettles. The wood fire under the giant kettles and the boiling apple butter combined to create a beautiful aroma that cascaded throughout town. Grandpa Becker was often known as "The Apple Butter Man."

My admiration for Dad is very deep, as I think back on the legacy he engraved in my heart. He passed away a couple of years ago at the age of 74. He set a precedent for future Becker husbands to outwardly show their wives love and affection. He romanced my mother in plain view of us boys. He kissed her affectionately when he strode through the back door and into the kitchen at about six o 'clock each night after work. We would take our designated places around the kitchen table meals to see and hear Mom question, listen, and encourage Dad's business deal while enjoying one of her homemade delicious suppers. There was a beautiful and respectful life of love being lived out by my parents in our two story century home on 20 East Main Street in Apple Creek.

Dad always spoke with a tone of admiration and respect for our mother. He danced with her in the dining room to the sounds of his beloved big band music. He always complimented her strengths and had a tendency to overlook her weaker traits. He did the same for me that allowed a self-conscious boy to be molded into what I trust is a compassionate, encouraging, and loving husband, father, and pastor. Somehow, Dad had learned that a home lacking in demonstrable love often times resulted in insecurity within the family. I truly appreciate the living legacy that he left for us.

Doug, the youngest of the Becker boys, seems to have spent his childhood memorizing my jaunts of enjoying the delight of youth. Even today, when gathered as family and friends, Doug will launch into a long and typically embarrassing re-telling of one of my childhood escapades with convincing precision. Most of those early childhood stories he tells are lost in the recesses of my mind. I like to think that I was too busy enjoying life to consider taking the time to memorize it all.

My brother Gerry is a couple years older than me. As the oldest, he was the most responsible of us Becker boys. He was also much more dedicated to those things he undertook. I, of course, was the bothersome younger brother that would routinely intrude on Gerry and his friends. My intrusions didn't subside even when they sped away on their bikes. Their peddling power far exceeded that of my own. As you might imagine, I eventually tracked down Gerry and his friends to their great disappointment and frustration.

It would often be that way for my older brother. If he wanted to find me, all he had to do was look over his shoulder. He unwittingly served as my most influential and motivating mentor. Gerry has always remained a step ahead of me throughout life and in career matters as well.

He married well and along with his wife, Sally, raised two beautiful, polite, and highly accomplished children, a boy and a girl. His children embody the dreams of their dad who grew up a financial underdog and the high school kid that came up just short of many of his desires and goals at the time. Nonetheless, he was a superior student and gifted trumpet player and thespian.

I recall one heartrending afternoon at the Waynedale High School's Golden Bear wrestling practice. Gerry was a strong and powerful senior wrestler, while I was a skinny freshman wrestler that would lose every non-varsity match I wrestled that year.

Gerry's weight class was comprised of some of the finest athletes in our school. In order to wrestle in the varsity match that week, Gerry would have to win this wrestle off. This was a win or lose match that he desperately wanted to win. His little brother watched hidden from view, but nearby. I was filled with emotion for my older brother who was among the youngest guys in his grade.

Gerry was powerfully sculpted from the long summer days he spent digging trees at our widowed grandmother's evergreen tree farm. Her name was Lucille Smith. Grandpa Floyd Smith, who was revered by all that met him, died in his mid-50's due to heart attacks, and eventually a debilitating stroke that left him helpless in a hospital bed in the spare bedroom. He had risen from depression era poverty to pay his way through college and become a teacher, school principal, award winning insurance salesman and, ultimately, entrepreneur of an evergreen farm. During that first semester of teaching, the school was so poor they could only pay him in chickens, which he graciously and thankfully accepted.

It was Grandpa Smith through whom a strand of creativity would be passed throughout his lineage. He was known to write poetry and prose. He was highly accomplished at whatever he did, no doubt due to his strong work ethic. He was a man's man that also appreciated the delicacies of life. He showered my Grandma Smith with love and affection.

Grandpa provided well for our grandmother and made beautiful and educational memories for his grandchildren in spite of his limited number of years this side of heaven. Memories of climbing up on Grandpa's lap for a tractor ride after a hard day in the fields remain fresh in my mind. His broad smile while lifting us up into the tractor seat, safely protected between his legs, is a picture that I'll always remember. We were thrilled, as was he, to meander throughout the evergreens on that big red Farmall tractor. Throughout the trip that allowed us to be one-on-one with our revered grandfather was an opportunity for us to sense his affection, passion, and knowledge. As he gently and purposefully guided the tractor throughout the farm, he told us about the various types of trees and other plants of nature we saw along the way.

Following this strong, middle aged man's stroke, I recall Grandpa Smith helplessly ringing the bell at his bedside to alert Grandma that he was in need of her assistance. Without Grandpa, our grandmother was left to operate the farm. Though she was a lady advancing in years, she would be by our side wrapping trees after Gerry dug them out. I would carry the trees to the nearby red four wheel drive GMC pickup truck.

Gerry was a beast at removing the trees from the firm Ohio ground in which hundreds of trees were planted. Each tree he dug would come out of the ground with roots cut by the sharp blade of his filed shovel edge in a round ball of dirt that Grandma, while in her late 50's or early 60's, would wrap in burlap and twine. Sometimes he would dig dozens of trees a day. Typically, temperatures were high and the sweat poured off his brow. These were some of the most magical days of our young lives.

When Grandma received a particularly large order of trees, our cousins, Tod, Paul, Don, and Stanley would join us for work on the tree farm. This would be welcome relief to spread the workload across a greater number of workers. But, more importantly, it meant our lunch time touch football games would have plenty of players.

After Grandma's delicious and huge mid-day lunches, we would head out to her front yard and play an energetic game of touch football. Afterward, we would collapse in utter exhaustion and take a half hour nap. Then it was back into the fields to work and have a few adventures. Did you know if a snake has a huge lump in the middle of its long slinky body that it just might have consumed a toad for a late afternoon snack? You would only know that by slicing the snake in half with a razor sharp shovel edge and seeing the toad crawl out of the guts of the snake and hop away. One dead snake, one saved toad.

The wrestle-off of Gerry's was an epic battle between my brother and the popular and gifted athlete that was his opponent. The match was very close. Gerry wrestled hard, much as he worked in those hot fields of trees. Nonetheless, to my gut wrenching dismay, he lost that match. It was as if I was on the mat with my brother. His disappointment was written across his devastated face. We both hurt; but neither of us spoke of that match then or since.

Gerry was your typical late bloomer and, as an adult, far surpassed the success of his classmates and friends. This is no doubt because of the work ethic carved in his psyche in the fields of our Grandmother's evergreen tree farm.

He also put his faith in the Lord as a teenager at Grace Youth Camp at Upper Silver Lake, Michigan. He was vital to the leadership of our church youth group where he excelled as a student-leader. Our Calvary Chapel church youth group swelled in numbers surpassing all expectations. In turn, many adults began coming to Calvary Chapel because their teens were attending.

I would be remiss to not include my first cousins in this review of those that had great influence in carefree childhood days. Elaine Robinson was Mom's older sister. She was married to Jack, who in his later years, would be recognized as a highly accomplished builder of 18th century furniture recreations. Actually his profession is as a joiner. Uncle Jack is an expert in dovetail work and uses precisely fitted joints, glue, and pegs to secure one piece of wood to another. Uncle Jack is just like the craftsmen of old who created perfectly fitted natural wood works of functionality and art.

The Robinson kids in sequence of oldest to youngest were Mick, Kathy, Lynne, Tod, and Sally. They were more like brothers and sisters to us. We spent most of our summer days together. The Robinsons lived a short drive from Calvary Chapel in the brick ranch home their Dad built. All of our church activities were done together.

Mick became our Calvary Chapel youth group pastor. Mick was cool and adventuresome, but passionate about leading teenagers to a personal relationship with Jesus Christ. Tod, who was less than a year older than myself was yet another great friend. Kathy and Sally were always in the mix as we dove into our adventures. But it was Lynne, who was just a year older than Tod, to whom I grew closest. She was the goofiest, brightest, most creative force I have or will ever encounter. Her crazy stunts and zest for life served to make each moment an unexpected explosion of creative thought.

Lynne was the big sister in my life. She was a thoroughly devoted Christian that used her God given talents in so many creative ministry efforts from her teen years and throughout her entire life. For more than 30 years she directed our church Bible camp. Camp was a week at nearby Camp Y-Noah that functioned in the same way that Grace Youth Camp in Western Michigan had done for us in our teen years. Untold numbers of young people have heard and responded to the Good News of salvation in Jesus Christ as a result of Lynne's leadership of Camp Berean Way.

Lynne was also at the forefront of a church ministry we call "Night in Bethlehem." Through her imaginative vision she brought to life an interactive scene depicting the streets of first century Bethlehem. Each Christmas season, Calvary Chapel presents "Night in Bethlehem" to share the true meaning of Christmas. Well over 1,000 visitors sojourn the recreated streets of Bethlehem to sense and feel how it might have been the night of Jesus' birth.

It was the encouragement of Lynne's husband, Dave Pahler that set the idea of writing this book in motion. Lynne had just tragically passed away while in her mid-50's after a five year battle with breast cancer. I sure wish she would have written that series of children's books she had dreamt up in her head, but never put to writing. So this book is a result of my boundless love and respect for Lynne (Robinson) Pahler who was valiant in her battle with cancer.

Chapter 2
Faith is the Victory

*Because everyone who is born from God defeats the world. And this is the victory that has defeated the world: our faith.*1 John 5:4(CEB)

It was a Norman Rockwell childhood filled with exploring, games, and mischief as our neighborhood friends and I freely enjoyed every crevice of our little home-town village. Our town of less than a thousand people was our land, awaiting discovery. Our playground included the street on which we skateboarded, the railroad bridge in which we hid, the creek where we fished, and the neighborhood pools where we swam. Our little village of Apple Creek was a boy's land of adventure.

The adventures were just as exciting when we were with the Robinson clan. There were backyard baseball games, swimming in the huge sand-lined lake at Clay's Park resort, hide and seek at night, and wild seven-man toboggan runs down the steepest hill known to man. With the toboggan filled to capacity we rocketed down the hill, through the valley and, on a good run, into the far off creek.

In those pre-computer days, games were physical in nature. They varied by the season and included kids from throughout the neighborhood. There was no parental organization to our baseball, football, basketball, and World War II re-enactment games. They were suggested, planned, and played by us kids. There were rules to follow, self-regulated conduct, and clear-cut winners and losers.

In contrast to the sophisticated and highly regulated standards of today, there were minimal safety concerns. A scratch or bruise was not of consequence, and I can't say I recall any tears due to hurt feelings. In retrospect, it is obvious the providential preparation these early days provided for the arduous journey that was to come.

Two defining moments of those pre-teen years were punctuated by the deadly reality of cancer.

Path of the Flesh

My best friend at the time, Hal, was the oldest son of Butch and Peggy who were friends of my parents. Our parents were friends dating back to school days. However, as a kid, I could sense a difference between my parents and Hal's. Quite simply, Hal and his family had a lot more fun stuff. His dad seemed to be quite wealthy, as a result of his truck driving position for Sugardale Meats. Yet, unlike my dad, Butch didn't wear a suit and tie. Plus, our Sunday mornings were different due to my family's time spent going to church.

I could sense that Butch and his buddies centered their gatherings on beverages in dark bottles and the smoking of cigarettes. All of this was foreign and somewhat intimidating to me. On occasion, dad would light up his aromatic pipe filled with Cherry Blend tobacco; but, I never saw my dad drink a bottle of beer. In my innocence, I sensed a darkness that was uncomfortable when I encountered Hal's dad and his friends as they gathered to drink, smoke, and laugh through life.

Hal's family built a new modern ranch home, had fancy reel-to-reel tape recorders, a brick fireplace upstairs and down, a real pinball machine, and best of all... the entire series of Dr. Seuss books. When I stayed overnight with Hal, I would awaken early to read "The Cat in the Hat," "One Fish, Two Fish," and "Put me in the Zoo." They just seemed to have all the stuff a family could ever dream to possess, most of which, we didn't have at home. Yet, I never sensed that we were being deprived because of what we didn't have. I simply enjoyed the things which were in Hal's possession. However, I had a fleeting thought ... *for all the incredible gifts that were showered on my friend; he had no interest or appreciation in them.*

Then, something very traumatic came crashing into full and terrifying reality. Though my parents wisely withheld the details to protect my naïveté, I could feel the fear that suddenly took hold of my parents and their friends. I pity the kid whose parents share too much of life's detailed hardships before their youthful emotions are matured. I would eventually learn that Butch had something called a brain tumor. A terrible intruder entwined his brain and offered no surgical or treatment options.

To this day, I can feel the fear as I did then in my 10 year old mind. My recollection is vivid when I walked into the basement of their newly constructed brick ranch to see Butch and his buddies gathered around the brick fireplace in the basement recreation room, beers in hand, cigarettes lit. Butch hollered out a greeting to me and I mumbled back a weak boyish response. In spite of my sense of boyish frailty, it seemed to me these men were more frightened of the gathering than me.

It was as if those very hard and tough men had nothing to offer their doomed and dying friend but nervous laughs, eyes filled with fear, and anesthetized feelings. Meanwhile, it was Butch who was seemingly bringing comfort, though he was the one living in the midst of the grip of a distressing disease. He was demonstrating strength through weakness.

The funeral for Hal's dad would follow within weeks of this memory. I still make it a point to drive past Butch's gravestone when at the Apple Creek cemetery.

Though the wound on my soul is no longer fresh, it's as if pulling open a scab that can still bleed with sorrow when I study Butch's small gravestone and witness the beginning and end with but 31 years between. His given name is framed by chiseled bouquets, as if hoping for tender mercies to be showered in his memory. The small inscription below speaks of a youthful widow whispering, "In loving memory."

Not long after his passing, Mom assured me that in his final days, Butch had come to what she confidently described as a relationship with Jesus Christ. She explained that his faith would result in him going to heaven. Though dumbfounded by the grief of all that had flashed into a seemingly perfect life, her words gave me a sense of bearing in which my young mind could find comfort. Her faith conveyed an assurance that gave hope in the midst of my confusion.

Subsequently, the gregarious and carefree brick home on the west edge of town became solemn and quiet after the funeral. Of all my memories of that terrible time I most recall the calming assurance that Mom conveyed to me about Butch's heavenly home. A seed was planted in my Spirit by her words and demeanor that would take hold for the personal storms that would become my reality.

Path of the Spirit

A few months after the puzzling and jolting reality that we would never again see or hear Hal's dad, this hideous scourge called cancer would target an even more fragile and soft spirit. One of our own, Ricky, who was a 12-year-old neighborhood buddy known for his artistic abilities and easy smile was said to be sick with something called leukemia. Although I was not as close with Ricky as I was with Hal, he was one of the neighborhood kids that was a couple years older than me. He astonished us with his sketches of the "Peanuts" comic strip characters. He could draw Charlie Brown, Snoopy, Linus and Lucy, and the whole gang with perfection. There was no doubt our friend possessed an incredible gift unlike any other kid we knew.

As I search my 11-year-old memories that are now 44-plus years in the past, I recall a kind and gentle boy. Born in a rough and tumble family on the far east side of town, Ricky had a special presence of calm, what I would now define as a generous and loving spirit with no malice for anyone or anything. He was fun, a delight to have around, and the picture of childhood innocence. Now, our buddy was in the clutches of a merciless disease that brutally consumed and destroyed this innocent kid. I can remember hearing from a neighbor friend about the effects that the leukemia and life-draining chemotherapy had upon his body.

Ricky was dead at the age of 13. It was barely a beginning to life as compared to Butch who had a seemingly full 31 years of life. This special Spirit that oozed from Ricky's soul was a memorable encounter with a person possessing unwavering faith in God. Though I don't recall the details, I can still sense the comforting Spirit that could be seen in Ricky's eyes. No wonder that his little gravestone is etched with a couple floral bouquets with his name, Richard Lynn, 1955-1968 inscribed on an open Bible.

Yet again, I had witnessed strength through weakness while living in the midst of the clutches of cancer.

Responding in Faith to Societal Chaos

Within two years, at the age of 11, I had encountered cancer caused death, cutting short life barely before it had begun. Meanwhile, the newscasters on television and radio solemnly reported the brutal murders of our President, his brother, and a non-violent leader for equality. And word of a hapless and confusing war in a far off country called Vietnam cascaded across our black and white television screen.

Dead American soldiers were reported by Walter Cronkite, said to be the most trusted news man in America. The numbers on the CBS television news network were recorded on a tote board, seemingly with no consideration for mourning the lost futures of the young American boys whose lives and dreams had just been snuffed out.

The streets of our cities were filled with race riots, and violent protests were common as the youth of America challenged anyone over the age of 30. Escapism through the illegal drug culture spawned music that invited experimentation with mind-altering substances. My Norman Rockwell enclave was unraveling in our village and throughout the nation. Simple dreams of joyful living were succumbing to angry and brutal consequences in the midst of wanton violence and death.

My parents, Larry and Eloise Becker, were perplexed by the horrors that were creating havoc on the orderly fabric of our society. Their concern was for the future of their young children. The church they had been attending seemed to be wandering in search of its mission and, increasingly, was suggesting social solutions to what my parents perceived to be a spiritual struggle within the heart of our national psyche. When they saw that our Sunday School curriculum was the "Weekly Reader" they inherently knew that they must search out a new church home that offered something far more substantive than mere manners and good deeds.

This seeking of a new church home would be birthed in an unusual and unique way in a 1960's culture dominated by traditional church denominations. People that went to church did not refer to themselves as Christians. Instead, they referred to themselves as Episcopalians, Methodists, Baptists, Roman Catholics, and other popular denominations. Each denomination had a somewhat different approach to what they believed.

Truth in Scripture

Mom's older sister, Elaine Robinson, and her husband, Jack, had begun a Bible study in the living room of their home on Tuesday evenings with a young pastor/teacher from England. He had served in the Royal Military Police in Italy and, along with his family, had also worked in evangelism. This young gentleman was Henry Hudson, and he had come to the U.S. to study at Milwaukee Bible Institute. Pastor Hudson and his loving wife, Shirley, had brought their family of three young blonde-haired children to Massillon, Ohio. Henry taught history at the local Christian university and served as a part time pastor at a little Baptist church in the small village of Newman.

Henry astonished the Bible study participants with his teaching of how to understand the Bible. Pastor Hudson emphasized that the entire Bible was truly reliable. It meant exactly what was written. Every word was God-breathed which meant the Bible was inspired by God Himself. The individual authors were merely human instruments that recorded in written form the things of God.

Pastor Hudson defended each of his teachings by supporting them with the Holy Scriptures literally and directly from the Bible. He showed how the Bible fit together as a literal and historically factual book of books. There were no contradictions within the 66 books or the 40-plus writers over 1500 years. He presented in his teaching the truths he gleaned during his education at Milwaukee Bible Institute (now known as Grace Bible College) and his own exhaustive and daily study of Holy Scripture. Pastor Hudson would become Dr. Hudson when he completed his Doctorate of Divinity degree.

As a young lad, Henry grew up on the rough side of London, England. He lived through the Nazi blitz during World War II. His childhood was rough and tumble, as he survived the culture of the streets and the brutal and ruthless bombings by Hitler's air force. He came to faith in Jesus Christ as a hardened teen who was a phenomenon at the snooker table. This expertise resulted in young Henry becoming a champion pool player in the nearby pubs. On occasion, he hustled money from competitors in the various pubs and pool halls in the rough-house ghetto in which he spent his formative years. He even managed to win the All-London teenage championship and become runner-up in the United Kingdom competition.

A freak accident that cut the tips of the fingers on his left hand sent young Henry to a Christian Hospital where a kindly British nurse cared for him physically and shared with him the salvation available to him through a personal relationship with Jesus

Christ. This was not a call to religion; it was a call to a personal relationship with God.

Henry accepted the salvation of Jesus Christ which covers the sins of the world, including our own past, present, and future sins. Wisely, upon accepting Jesus Christ as his personal Savior, the nurse told young Henry he must go tell someone what he had done. As he walked back into the hospital ward, a rebellious buddy, upon seeing his face, exclaimed: "Not you Henry! Not you!"

Yes, Henry had indeed stepped out in faith to believe in Jesus Christ as his personal Savior. This was a thoroughly transforming life event for Henry that led him into a lifetime of pastoral ministry and historical teaching. He would join Britain's Royal Military Police, which provided post-World War II order to Trieste, Italy. Many of his fellow soldiers would accept Christ through his testimony and persuasion of the Holy Spirit. They would spend a lifetime in ministry, whether through the pastorate or in the course of their respective business endeavors.

Pastor Hudson explained an important component of Biblical understanding to the Bible study participants in Jack and Elaine's living room. He emphasized the necessity of knowing the audience and the context of the biblical passage. We should know, for instance, if the passage was written to the Jews or the Gentiles. Henry emphasized the unique ministry of the Apostle Paul who was called to be the apostle to the Gentiles. Have you ever wondered why the 12 disciples limited their ministry to Israel? Why didn't they take the good news of Jesus Christ into the entire world? Why did Paul come on the scene and become one of the primary authors of the New Testament after the four Gospels of Matthew, Mark, Luke, and John?

In the gospels, the focus of the writers is on God's chosen people, the Jews. The Gentiles of the day were considered mere secondhand citizens, spiritually speaking. In fact, they were often called "dogs." An understanding of the Holy Scriptures is greatly enhanced when a Christian realizes the unique Gospel of Grace that Paul was chosen by God to reveal to all people, Jew and Gentile alike.

The Gospel of Grace

Paul's given name was Saul, after the first King of Israel. As a young adult, he was molded and developed into an unmatched Jewish pedigree. His hometown was Tarsus, a free city of Rome with a significant Jewish population. At the age of 14, his proud father sent him to Jerusalem to be taught by the great rabbi teacher, Gamaliel.

Paul was a gifted and hungry student. He was zealous in his faith. He believed in the law of the prophets that Saul had been taught, and he fervently believed Jesus to be a blasphemer. Paul was so dedicated to this belief that he was arresting, jailing, and even sending to execution anyone that claimed to be a believer in Jesus Christ.

It was this zealous Jew who we first hear about in Acts 7 of the New Testament. Paul was holding the cloaks of the mob while they stoned Stephen to death. Further details in the Bible state Saul was on the road to Damascus to arrest and jail more believers, when Jesus Christ literally knocked him to the ground and called out, "Why are you persecuting me?" Saul would be blinded for three days as a result of this encounter with the living Christ. Later, God would use this zealous antagonist of Christ and mold him into His special messenger to the Gentile nations.

Not only was Paul's message primarily to Gentiles, but also to the Jews that they would believe in their Messiah, Jesus "The Christ", the anointed one. His given name was Jesus. His title was Christ. Jesus Christ was the God/man, 100 percent God, 100 percent man. These statements were blasphemy to the Jewish people when they heard them.

Jesus, known for His humble lineage and backwoods upbringing, was telling the religious elite of the day that He was God in the flesh. And when Jesus "The Christ" claimed to be God, His own chosen people of those times would not receive Him as their prophesied and promised Messiah. Instead, the Jews of the day demanded that Jesus Christ be crucified. He did go willingly to His death on the cross of Calvary. When He died, Jesus not only died a brutal and hostile death physically but, more importantly, He died as the "Lamb of God" who takes away the sins of the world.

As you read the Old Testament, you will see that the Jewish people came to the great Temple of God in Jerusalem to sacrifice animals, such as a lamb, to temporarily cover their sins. But, because the lamb was not "The Perfect Lamb," the Jews had to return during the feast days at the same time each year to offer their sacrifices to a perfect God.

Jesus was, and is, the perfect Lamb of God. The Son of God, who was sent by His Father, was the fulfillment of the law. Jesus was dispatched by His Heavenly Father to come to earth as a mere baby, born in Bethlehem to rescue and reconcile us. God gave up His Son to mankind to do as they pleased, simply because God loves us so much.

The Bible states that all of us are sinners; all fall short of God's perfection. None of us are good enough to measure up to the perfection of God. So, we need the "Lamb of God", a Savior who is Christ the Lord. Just as God required the blood of lambs to temporarily cover sins, God required the blood of the Perfect Lamb, Jesus, to cleanse us of our sins permanently.

Pastor Hudson was teaching this truth to his Bible study participants and it was being supported with the writings found in the Bible. Truly, they were learning that the Bible did not require interpretation to understand. Every page of the Bible was reliably accurate and written for them. The Gospel of Grace was written for Gentile and Jew co-equally. The Apostle Paul was the Apostle to the Gentiles.

In the third chapter of Paul's letter to the Ephesians, he describes his unique ministry as preaching "The Mystery." The mystery is that this Gospel of Grace, rather than the concept that we work toward making ourselves clean in front of a Holy God to live up to the law in our own efforts, is available as a gift from Jesus Christ to be received by Jew and Gentile alike, who are now co-heirs of the Kingdom of God.

It was a mystery, because none of the Old Testament prophets had ever spoken or written of this Gospel of Grace that was now available to all mankind. Anyone who believed this Gospel could go to heaven, no one was excluded. The Gentile no longer had to go through the Jew for his salvation. We are now made clean in the presence of a Holy God by believing that Jesus Christ is the Messiah.

He Stands at Your Door

The Bible states that the Lord stands at the door of your heart and knocks to see if you will let Him enter your life. Jesus, in his kindness and grace, allows us to accept Him or deny Him. We have the free will to accept, ignore, or reject His ever-present knock on our door. This is the heart of the good news that churches are to preach and teach. This gospel unifies, it does not divide into separate sub-groups.

This understanding by the religiously eclectic Bible study group comprised of Methodists, Episcopalians, Baptists, Church of Christ members, etc. clicked in the hearts and minds of each member of the Bible study.

Most of the participants had initially appeared at the Bible study to be polite, because of the enthusiastic invitation they had received from my Aunt Elaine. The first thing they realized was few of them had brought a Bible. So, they searched the Robinson household for Bibles for each of the attendees. Imagine needing a Bible for an in-home Bible study! The first question of the night: "So, how does the Bible say that a person is saved?"

Pastor Hudson had the participants of the Bible study open their Bibles to Romans 10:9-10 (CEB) where the Apostle Paul clearly states: *Because if you confess with your mouth "Jesus is Lord" and in your heart you have faith that God raised him from the dead, you will be saved. Trusting with the heart leads to righteousness, and confessing with the mouth leads to salvation.*

Subsequently, this little in-home Bible study, under the guidance and direction of something truly supernatural, became an independent, non-denominational community Bible church in Massillon, Ohio. It was the intent of these 25 founding members that this church would serve as a testimony to the Gospel of the Grace of God. Miraculously, Calvary Chapel has done just that for nearly 50 years now.

Chapter 3
Formative Years

As for parents, don't provoke your children to anger, but raise them with discipline and instruction about the Lord. Ephesians 6:4 (CEB)

Our formative years set the stage for the rest of our lives. The relationships we establish, the character we develop, the faith we accept, the behavior we carry out, the opportunities we seize… all of these are mortared together to establish foundation for our adult years. We as parents are called to mentor and mold our children throughout their formative years so they can be a blessing to their family, friends, and community. By parenting our children to serve others before self we are raising children that are honoring to all.

Personal Faith and Failure

As my teen years began, my passion for playing sports grew insatiably. The physicality of the various games we played gave me a kind of euphoria that filled my soul with satisfaction and a thirst for tough competition. I came to relish the challenge of each sport and especially enjoyed the feeling of triumph because, in our neighborhood, I was typically the youngest of the competitors; an underdog to win.

Correspondingly, those early teen years would give birth to my personal faith relationship with Jesus Christ. This spiritual part of my life journey would bloom and become my own at Grace Youth Camp which was affiliated with Grace Bible College. It was a real adventure for me to pack up in a bus with kids my own age from different parts of the Great Lakes region. We enjoyed the adventurous seven hour trip to the week-long youth camp. Grace Youth Camp was dedicated to presenting the gospel of the grace of God to teenagers. It was an adventure away from parents and our everyday surroundings.

We stayed in A-frame cabins with bunk beds. We shared a bathroom for the 12-15 boys per cabin. The girls were in their own group of A-frame cabins on the opposite side of camp. We were surrounded by the sand dunes of upper Western Michigan. Sunshine-filled days with a balance of fun activities and heart challenging devotional and chapel events were uniquely presented to relate to teens growing into maturity. Our style of music was sung to the accompaniment of guitars and drums.

All of this was done in the midst of the early 70's culture that was saying "forget about delayed gratification, just grab the emotional rush of the day." The lifestyle of "live for today and for your self-satisfaction" washed over our generation with devastating consequences. It was at Grace Youth Camp that I expressed my desire to follow a different path. My faith journey would be born there in the comfortable bubble of like-minded Christian teens. Standing strong for that faith would be harder at home and in school with my friends. After all, among my peers at home, I just wanted to fit in and have fun.

As family, much of our time together was spent at Calvary Chapel. The church was much more than just a place we checked into for an hour on Sunday mornings with a quick escape to return to the same old lifestyle. The group of young parents attending those Tuesday night Bible studies faced the seemingly impossible task of buying, renovating, and maintaining a real, functioning church building.

To our amazement, 62 folks attended the first Sunday morning Calvary Chapel worship service on July 5th, 1964. But, before this miraculous worship service could take place in the abandoned Methodist church on 8th Street SW in Massillon, there was work to be done. The task of restoring the old church building would require hours of painting, remodeling, cleaning, and significant sweat equity that was lovingly poured into the effort. It was my first encounter with a spirit-driven dream that beat the odds.

No matter how old or young, everyone helped. This group did not shy away from using its physical abilities and work trades for the establishment of a structure. This building would contain members who would reach out in love rather than yelling, confrontation, and destruction. The idea was to build something that provided answers to the confusing times that were overwhelming the current culture. The experience brought about a strong unity among the people.

The inspiration for the efforts was not the renovation of a building, but the excitement to share a new-found appreciation for understanding the Word of God. It was an answer to a world spiraling into ever greater confusion and brokenness.

One particular event from those early days of Calvary Chapel happened as I was working outside of Pastor Henry Hudson's church study as a young boy. I could hear his distinctively rich baritone voice as he was practicing the singing of the hymns for Sunday worship. Here was a man singing with great gusto and sincerity, who had no knowledge of my ability to hear him. That simple act impressed upon this pre-teen boy that this was an adult filled with sincerity and substance. Henry was a man of unusual zeal for the Lord. He did not preach one thing and live another. He was genuine when many people were being revealed as phonies and fakes. This guy meant what he said and said what he meant. Henry was confident, straightforward, and scripturally grounded in a society that was increasingly unsure of any grounding in final truth or authority.

Through our church, I learned of this teenage haven called Grace Youth Camp. It was there that I sensed it was important for me to take personal ownership of my Christian faith. This faith was not something that could be passed down to me by family, friends, or some kind of church ceremony. By means of what I was hearing in the church choruses we sang, the Sunday School lessons we had, and Pastor Hudson's sermons, it was clear that it was my personal choice to open the door at which Jesus Christ stood, patiently knocking, awaiting my response.

This path of faith began at the conclusion of a particularly soul challenging message at camp. Thereafter, I got up from my seat and stepped forward to the platform to acknowledge I had accepted Jesus Christ as my personal Savior. It was my idea and my personal commitment. I concluded that, based on what was written in the Bible, our personal entrance into heaven was not achieved in whole or part by my good works. Rather, I learned through our fledgling church and this youth camp that salvation is totally of the Lord as he fully completed the forgiveness of my sins on the cross at Calvary. This personal response to a supernatural calling on my 13 year old life was a defining moment that would establish a strong, unwavering foundation on which my adulthood would be secure and miraculously sustained.

Dancing in Deception

One memory comes to mind from those long ago elementary school days. A school dance had been scheduled for the fifth and sixth grade boys and girls. It was this young boy's desire to be a participant in a sure sign of leaving behind childish things for the passionate pursuit of the loveliness of the fairer gender. In other words, I was crazy for girls.

All those dreams of dancing beneath the dimmed gymnasium lights to the soundtrack of my youth, with popular hits by *The Association*, *Tommy James and the Shondells*, and *The Beatles*, came to a crashing end when my parents would not permit me to attend the dance. They protested to the school administration that a dance for kids at such an early age would only serve to encourage mischievous behavior.

Seemingly, my parents were the only puritans among the entire community. The thought of not participating in this passage into maturity created a desire to deceive, so I could dance in my youthful delight.

In my young mind, I conceived a plan of deception. On the evening of the dance, I would ask to camp out in our tents down by the creek with the neighbor boys. We had done this on a regular basis, so I was sure I would be granted permission. I was given the approval, and I would leave our campsite at nightfall for the elementary school on the hill. As I walked in the door dressed in my fashionable jacket of the late 60's, the music and atmosphere intoxicated my senses.

The gymnasium floor was flooded with students, moving to the music we heard on our favorite top 40 radio station. The on-stage record player amplified the music that moved the heart and soul of the late baby boomer generation. These young recording artists represented a break from the formality of the past to unleash an expression of youthful vibrancy through electric guitars, pulsating drums, and fresh, liberating vocals.

The rock and roll soundtrack of our youth created a furor among the big band generation, including my parents. The big band sounds had soothed the devastating reality of the horrors and tumult of World War II. The eloquence and highly professional sounds created by orchestras brought to life a laid back, relaxing sound. The inspiring, nostalgic music and lyrics were being replaced by a rebellious, progressive sound and message of a rowdy and unconstrained lifestyle.

In the midst of my deceitful participation in that forbidden dance, the school principal, to which my parents had protested, confronted me and wondered why I was there. I spewed another deceptive excuse and hurried out the back door and into the darkness of a fall night. I ran down the back alleys of town, hoping not to be noticed, while returning to our campsite. My heart was filled with anxiety as I imagined what would happen if I were found out. Though my fears were not realized, a tendency toward deceit for my own satisfaction would hinder the maturity and discipline required of a responsible and trustworthy young man.

Empty Pursuits

I don't want to look back on my early teen years with too much harsh judgment. I wasn't a juvenile delinquent. But, I was struggling to establish my identity. A few of us found a way to get cigarettes, and I had the supplier purchase a pack of Kool's without the filters for me. I thought that this would spread the word that I was pretty tough and rather cool myself, right? I think

I smoked about half of those hideous cancer sticks and got sicker than a dog. That was the end of my cigarette smoking.

Not long thereafter, I can remember Hal and I walking past "The Big Apple," a bar in town where the young drinkers gathered. Up the street, was the bar for the old time drinkers. As we passed a group of leather-clad guys near "The Big Apple," Hal said something that I could never imagine. Hal said he wanted to be just like those guys.

I couldn't believe it; my buddy flat out said his goal was to be a hoodlum?! I liked to have as much fun as anyone, but that lifestyle reminded me of the group of dark and helpless friends that I had seen impotently gathered around Hal's dad in his final days.

To my sad disappointment, Hal's goal would be realized and his life would devolve into a haze of narcotics, broken relationships, and an early death. Could that have been my destiny? Only by my acceptance of Jesus Christ as Savior did my destiny take a different path of clarity, faithfulness, and abundance in life.

Wilderness Wanderings

Those pre-teen years were preparing me for an impending change in my young life. Apple Creek Elementary school was a mere walk through downtown Apple Creek and up the sidewalk to the old familiar and comfortable school building for grades one through six, which had served as the high school for my parents. I felt safe in this place and especially enjoyed adventurous and reckless recesses on the big swing-set. We would veer from our left and right to crash into our buddies as we soared through the air on our favorite swing.

An unmotivated approach to studying grew with each passing grade. It was more exciting to sneak out of class as our teacher sat in the front of the room, seemingly dazed and oblivious to the conduct of her fifth grade students. During one memorable afternoon, more than half of us would stealthily sneak out the classroom door, unnoticed by our disengaged teacher. As if awakened from a conscious stupor, she finally looked up through her thick glasses to realize that the classroom before her, which had started as a room full of students, was now more than half empty. We had slipped past her gaze, snuck through the door and traveled down the hall to gather and giggle in the restroom. We exploded in gut-laughing glee from our cunning, unnoticed escape.

Fortunately, sixth grade brought Mr. Herb Broda into my school experience. He would be the catalyst for my growth and maturity as a student and young man. A first year teacher with a faith-filled heart, he was fresh out of college. Mr. Broda's teaching was unique and fun as he taught things, such as multiplying fractions, with a flair for learning those necessary basics with little songs. They were fun to remember and silly to sing. His enthusiasm for education and confidence in the potential of his students captured my interest in learning unlike any other school teacher I had known.

We became friends to be encouraged, rather than students to be embarrassed with red-penned failure. He was determined to treat us as individuals with potential, rather than another class of kids to be shuffled like cattle through endlessly boring classes.

The highlight was when Mr. Broda announced that he would take all of us sixth graders on an adventure to our nation's capital, Washington D.C. Cookbooks were created and sold, and dump trucks of newspapers were collected and recycled for money. With each Washington D.C. fundraising effort, we grew closer together as students, parents, and teachers. Before, I would trudge up the uneven sidewalk to our village elementary. Now, it was a joy to go to school.

Mr. Broda's idea of education was not confined by old, stodgy, tired educational practices. He brought learning into the world and community in which we lived. The biggest personal boost he gave was to assign me the duties of class secretary. Furthermore, he entrusted me to be a chaperone of our room in Washington, D.C. For the first time, a teacher was demonstrating that he had confidence in this unconfident boy.

It is this method of building a person's character and confidence that I continue to practice today. Mr. Broda opened my eyes to the principle that the best way to teach is by giving responsibility that stretches a student, while providing a reachable expectation. Initiative seems to be stifled by highly regulated, heavy handed oversight. Effective mentoring provides the encouragement to lead, and the grace to allow mistakes in small matters.

This approach best prepares the student to later take on big challenges with confidence. Kids deprived of these opportunities seem to be vulnerable to becoming inwardly self-conscious adults that avoid challenges, while settling for mediocrity in life. These formative years bathed in encouragement, responsibility, and the grace to allow messing up small matters set the stage for focused and fulfilling pursuits as an adult. By Mr. Broda's example, we learned the perfect antidote to wilderness wanderings. A mentoring approach absent of these characteristics leaves an empty and frustrated heart.

Sinking in Selfishness

Seventh grade meant leaving the comfortable and familiar Apple Creek Village Elementary School for a consolidated junior high school that brought together kids from four different neighboring communities. Fear filled my heart. There would be new teachers, unknown kids from other towns, and an unfamiliar building. I had heard of the harsh initiation to expect from the eighth grade boys. The confidence I had tasted through Mr. Broda was seemingly gone.

That fear would only serve to temporarily thwart my maturation. Fear led to unnecessary anxiety, which led to a sinking self-image and manifested itself in a truly awful academic performance. I felt rudderless in a mostly imagined sea of turmoil. All of this turned my perspective from others to self. The scourge of selfishness sunk my optimism as I began junior high school. I would eventually realize that this mindset is pervasive among kids and, more tragically, grown adults.

Chapter 4
Find Your Identity

But in all these things we win a sweeping victory through the one who loved us. Romans 8:37(CEB)

Flickers of hope began to grow out of a life that was being squandered in those junior high and high school days. A book report, being a part of a successful team, learning the perils of phoniness, becoming aware of blessings, and finding faithful friends lit a life through which the light of Christ could shine brightly.

A Life-Changing Book Report

The first change came as a result of a book report assignment. During library period, I searched for a book that I could consume with the same passion as those Dr. Seuss books on Hal's bedroom shelf. Fortunately, I came across one on the higher shelves of the library, a biography of the successful businessman and philanthropist Andrew Carnegie. As I read the hard-back book I was mesmerized by the philanthropy that would be his legacy. Carnegie expressed his passion for the value of reading by building a huge number of library buildings throughout the nation. He had parlayed his enormous success in the steel industry to strengthen the fabric of society. I loved the idea of personal gain bringing community edification. Everyone could benefit from Carnegie's gift, if only they would walk through the library door where an abundance of knowledge and encouragement awaited a person's discovery.

The second glimmer of growth was found on the Junior High football team. The many backyard pickup games and attending Friday night football games at Waynedale High School throughout my pre-teen and early teen years formed a dream to play under the lights in front of the proud community fans. It seemed everyone came together to fill the bleachers and cheer on the victory-rich Golden Bear football team. I was enamored by every aspect of the widely respected young men that wore the gold and brown uniforms.

The achievement of this dream would begin on the seventh grade football team, for which seemingly every boy tried out. It was heaven on earth to be issued those oversized, second-hand red shoulder pads, distinctive gold helmets, and team uniform. It quickly became evident that my dream was much bigger than the reality of my physical stature and athletic abilities. If I were to accomplish my heart-felt goal, it would have to be as a blocker for the swifter and more gifted players.

This reality of being a part of the team rather than a star of the team in no way dampened the fire that burned within to be a Golden Bear. On one memorable game day in the eighth grade, I was wearing my prized jersey in great anticipation of the game that would follow the school day. Very low on my thoughts were the classes I was enduring that day. As I sat in our predictably boring English class that was lacking of any creativity, we were being quizzed on diagramming sentences. My mind was filled with anticipation for what I considered much more important priorities.

How much would I play in the game? Would their guys be big and strong? Would I be over matched? My wandering thoughts were readily recognized by this teacher who cared for her cat far more than a mere football game. Suddenly in front of the entire class she put me to shame for my daydreaming ways which she correctly determined to be on the game, rather than her lesson. It only served to further hinder my motivation for academic success. Today the criticism is fresh while the game is lost to my memory. What a departure from the motivating and empowering methods used by Mr. Broda!

Double-Hearted

The overall fear and pessimism that washed over me would carry into my freshman year of high school which was comprised of grades 9-12. Entering high school meant another building transition and a return to the bottom of the hierarchy of school social status. Again, the fear of the potential for a belittling initiation fostered an unsettled heart. Surely the rumors of a group of senior boys forcing my head into a flushing toilet would be my humiliating reality.

That freshman year of high school came on the heels of my acceptance of Jesus Christ as my personal Savior at Grace Youth Camp during that supernatural week.

Back home as a freshman in high school, my heart was captivated with being a part of the "in" crowd. Meanwhile, I would spend a lot of time with the Calvary Chapel youth group. It became convenient due to the 25 mile separation between church and school to live a double-hearted lifestyle. Greg, the unprincipled, vulgar, tough guy at school. At the same time, presenting the mask of character, purity, and gentleness at Calvary Chapel on Sunday morning and while participating in youth group. The kids from school and church were comfortably separate, which allowed me to live as a double-hearted hypocrite. Inwardly, a battle raged within my Spirit. It was a lifetime lesson that, once called by God, a full and complete yielding of the heart is required. Otherwise, a difficult and winding road becomes our reality.

Talking the Walk

As might be your life experience, I increasingly learned the vocabulary of a personal walk with Christ. Yet, for all the talk, my walk was for myself rather than the Lord. This behavior surely fostered a false faith that gave little glory to the God of all good things.

The consequence was missed opportunities for sharing and experiencing the power and strength through the Spirit that could have guided me through my teenage years. Because of my lack of faith in all matters of life, a wound to my testimony of walking with Him exists today. Is it possible, dear reader, that beyond your affliction through which you or a loved one is enduring, you have merely learned to talk the walk of faith while doing the opposite?

Would you not agree that the psychological strain of masking our true heart only serves to establish a life weak at its foundation and lacking in abundant and confident living? In order to live in the midst of disease and distress, the lessons learned in those moments of challenge reveal the vital importance of a complete and transparent yielding to someone much bigger than ourselves. When pressed by our personal mortality, we soon experience that walking the walk of Christ strengthens our resolve. Meanwhile, mere words leave our true walk weak and lacking direction and power.

For all the anguished wailing and talk of courageous battles, overcoming disease and distress begins in silence and waiting. Our minds desire instant relief and escape from our thorn in the flesh. Living in the midst is found through the quiet of a firm foundation that allows us to live beyond our reach.

Blind to Blessings

As is often the case, a cascade of blessed relationships and experiences began to fill my high school experience. These would be blessings to which I was ignorant. In particular, the birth of a blessed relationship with my future wife would serve to be integral to my survival of cancer and resolve to thrive in spite of multiple life-threatening medical challenges that were to come.

Additionally, I found my confidence on the gridiron. My dream to be a Golden Bear football player became reality in my sophomore year. I had found a position through which I could excel. Coach Jack Chelf, the former Marine who coached the varsity team's linemen for the Golden Bear football team, had told me that if I perfected the art of long snapping for punts and field goals, then I might have the opportunity to play for the varsity as a sophomore in spite of my lack of size.

Coach Chelf's suggestion was all the encouragement I needed to prepare myself to win the long snapper position. Nearly every summer day, I could be found hiking the ball between my legs to a designated target. By the time summer football practices began, I had perfected the task of hiking the ball to the punter or field goal holder. My form was unconventional due to a lack of formal training; but, the results were the measure by which the position would be won.

True to his word, Coach Chelf named me the varsity long snapper for the Golden Bears after he witnessed the results of my summer of diligent practice. There were many more athletically gifted football players than myself. But, none had focused on practicing for this role with the same passion as I had. A blessed dream was realized because I wanted it more than anyone else on the team. It was a vital life lesson that focused determination can help you beat the odds.

Golden Opportunity

Although I played sparingly as a specialist snapping for punts and field goals as a sophomore, the coaches rewarded my contribution to the team by giving me a varsity letter. This honor was all the more valuable because it included me on the undefeated and league champion Golden Bear football team. It was extremely rare for a sophomore to earn a varsity letter in the highly successful Golden Bear football program. Such an honor was beyond the wildest expectations of a 15 year old boy longing to find a means to achieve a respected accomplishment and some form of personal identity.

The following summer would usher in a rite of passage for me and my 16 year old guy friends, specifically, Dave, Dennis, and Mike. We each passed our driving exam, which provided us the freedom to explore beyond our backyards. The odd collection of secondhand cars we drove did not diminish the sense of freedom that our driver's licenses provided.

Most of my friends played football, wrestled, and threw the shot and discus for the Golden Bears. The guys and I were always together, particularly Dennis, playing pick-up games or running through the village cemetery to get in shape. The cemetery was blocked in perfect quarter mile squares, which made for measurable timing as we sought to improve our speed. Of course, there were teenage adventures achieved and mischief lived out. But, no one got badly hurt as we reveled in our youth.

The friend that I spent the most time with was a farm kid named Dennis whose parents had sold the family farm and moved into Apple Creek. Dennis and I would spend nearly every day together from the summer we turned 16 until he left for college on an academic scholarship.

He would readily admit there were smarter kids in our class, but no one out worked Dennis when it came to his studies. He was peculiar among us athletes in his equally dedicated pursuit of academics. Throughout our friendship, I learned first-hand the power of the mind and spirit that could take a farm kid from a village of less than a thousand residents to a decorated Ph.D. and career as an accomplished scientist working closely with our U.S. Congress.

A Dream-Girl Further Motivates the Pursuit of Excellence

While my athletic successes began to be realized, my academics were still lagging behind. That was the case until the most beautiful, bright, and well-respected young lady came into my life. Of all the blessed dreams that could have occurred in my junior year of high school, I never imagined the blessing that I would fall into before the fall homecoming dance.

She was unquestionably one of the most beautiful girls in our junior class. Her natural beauty was only surpassed by her purity of character and outstanding scholarship. Surely a girl such as Debbie Spencer would never show an interest in an undistinguished boy such as me.

Nonetheless, my latest football achievement made me a full time starter for the varsity Golden Bear football team and bolstered my sense of confidence. My confidence continued to grow beyond my expectations. As I learned a few years earlier from Mr. Broda, achievements have a snowball effect. Accomplishments in one area of life typically spill over into another, and soon each challenge is overcome through a passionate pursuit of the desired result.

It was a beautiful, sunshine splashed early fall afternoon. School had just begun, and students involved in extra-curricular activities were responsible for blanketing the community to seek sponsors for our yearbook ads. Dennis and I had purchased what we thought to be the coolest velvet caps at the local discount store. The style and fabric of these caps screamed the 1970's culture of unusual and fashion-altering design.

As we cruised the small alleys and streets of Apple Creek, we were more interested in being seen than actually collecting money for the school. Indeed, we were seen by this young beauty named Debbie Spencer who was with her friend Rhonda.

To my stunning surprise, I heard Debbie Spencer say "yes" when I invited her to be my date to the October 1973 homecoming dance. Mere words cannot capture the blessings that continue to this day as a result of that unbelievable response by Debbie.

She was everything I wasn't, but desired to be. Debbie was restrained and quiet; I was carefree and loud. She was studious and meticulous; I would barely crack a book and was unorganized. She liked solitude; I was the life of the party. She was flat out gorgeous; I had a big nose. How in the world could such a girl have an interest in me? I would later learn that it was my walk of faith to which she was attracted, not my precious athletic prowess. One would grow deeper and stronger to this day, while the other would fade away.

More dates followed, and our relationship matured. This maturation took place mostly because I was motivated to measure up to Debbie's example. After all, a girl of this high reputation would not stay with a dumb jock. Thus, my pursuit of academics grew because I knew Debbie was among the smartest students in our class. Suddenly, those lessons that I had heard, but was too undisciplined to reveal through testing, became yet another pursuit that would compel me to reach beyond my limited expectations.

Little did I realize that the good Lord had bracketed me between a best friend of future determined scholastic accomplishment and a girlfriend with an undaunted spirit, bright mind, and a heart filled with loving care. It was a lesson of positive peer pressure that would foster a resolve that served me well, while living in the midst of the life storms that would soon appear on the horizon.

Chapter 5
Young Adult Adventures

But you must keep control of yourself in all circumstances. Endure suffering, do the work of a preacher of the good news, and carry out your service fully. 2 Timothy 4:5 (CEB)

Ah, the wonder of being a young adult excited to take on the world and make your mark. I trust that you entered your young adult years filled with anticipation for the journey that was ahead. Life is indeed filled with its share of ups and downs, twists and turns. It is to be seized rather than succumbed to. It is never too late to seize the day. Take up your sword and enter the fray. Bystanders will come to the end of things in a state of weakness without having tasted the joys or tears of truly living in strength.

The Exciting Beginning Together

Long summer days of painting houses had provided a nest egg to purchase the most opulent engagement and wedding rings I could afford at the downtown Wooster jewelry store. I so wanted to give my Debbie the lifestyle she deserved.

Prior to our engagement, I had begun pursuit of higher education at the local community college. I paid in cash from the hard-earned savings I had accumulated. Quarterly payments were made for classes in speech and communications, which I sensed were my career callings. The monies saved from painting houses in the summer provided the necessary tuition. While going to school, I had begun working for my parents at their newly-opened casual clothing retail store. To my further delight, I landed a part time announcer job at our local radio station, WWST in Wooster.

Meanwhile, Debbie's dad had encouraged her to attend a semester-long airline stewardess school two hours away in Pittsburgh, Pennsylvania. Our short-term separation only served to bolster my resolve to ask Debbie to marry me.

Now all of that waiting was in the past and we were anxious to enter an exciting future filled with optimistic expectations. It was my dream come true to have emerged from a self-conscious boyhood to a young, strong, and confident married man.

A Wedding in Faith

At the age of 21, Debbie and I were married in her little home church in the village of Fredericksburg, Ohio. October 7th, 1978 was a sunshine-filled fall day full of joyful expectation for the life to come for Debbie and me.

Our family and friends filled the wooden pews of the comfortable little sanctuary. My church youth group leader was playing the piano. My younger brother, Doug, would sing "The Lord's Prayer." My white long-tailed tux and Debbie's flowing white gown gave testimony to the bright future that awaited a popular young couple from the heart of the community.

Flowers were in order; everything was properly performed until we arrived at the altar. To our bewildering surprise, the minister was missing! Reverend Kerns had not been at the rehearsal practice the prior evening due to a case of the flu. His wife had assured us that he would be fine by the time of the wedding ceremony. The reality was the good reverend was home sick in bed rather than preparing to administer our nuptial vows.

As the processional music ended, an uncomfortable hush fell upon the people filling the sanctuary pews. I looked to my right and saw a look of stunned disbelief on the face of my friend, Randy Weaver, who now serves as a pastor to me and so many others. Some of our uncles would later tell us they were reaching for a Bible to perform the wedding vows themselves. With no sign of Reverend Kerns, and my future father-in-law and bride awkwardly standing with me in front of the full church, I whispered to my brother to sing "The Lord's Prayer" to buy us some time. Fortunately, as Doug concluded his song, the reverend slipped in the side door and took his place before us.

Surely, this served as a harbinger of unexpected surprises to come in our married life.

Honeymoon Scare

Well, this begins the part of my letter to you that I prefer not to re-live. But, it's probably what we have in common.

I first noticed, while honeymooning at Disney World, a slight pain. The discomfort seemed to subside as we spent the remaining few days of our honeymoon in Disney, before heading to Paradise Island in the Bahamas for a week. Upon our arrival at our hotel on Paradise Island, a storm had just passed leaving a tumultuous surf. Our inexperience with ocean waves gave us a sense that this was the normal surf that was to be expected.

So, with no familiarity with the powerful undertow caused by the departing storm, we headed into the ocean naive to the danger. Not long into our first swim in an ocean, Debbie was torn from my grasp by a crashing wave and momentarily caught in the powerful undertow of the receding waters. It seemed to take an eternity before I could catch Debbie by the arm and pull her from the strong grasp of the stormy waters. Little did we know the ominous seas that life had in store for us in our first year of marriage.

After arriving safely at home, we gathered with family in our rented home to open the multitude of wedding gifts that were piled high in the cozy living room. Even today, it churns my stomach to recall the weeks of innocence we enjoyed before the entrance of the deadly elephant in the room. It was amazing to be living out a dream as a married couple. What a joy it was to stay with Debbie after needing to leave for home each evening during our five years of dating. It was, indeed, what they would call wedded bliss with the girl I never imagined would say "yes" to my proposal.

Prepared for the Unexpected

Up to this point in my life, the most significant medical situation had been an elbow dislocation which occurred during a high school varsity wrestling match. There was also a recollection of Mom explaining that I had scarlet fever as a young kid. Otherwise, my total experience with the American medical system involved routine doctor visits, a fall from my bicycle that tore up the skin on my right knee, and that one emergency room visit to resolve my elbow issue.

After our marriage I was added to Debbie's group health insurance plan. Her account clerk job at Apple Creek Developmental Center provided a comprehensive and generous program through Blue Cross/Blue Shield.

Little did I know the vital importance of this seemingly routine eligibility for a healthcare plan for someone as vigorous and healthy as me.

Chapter 6
Enter the Elephant

So then, I ask you not to become discouraged by what I'm suffering for you, which is your glory. Ephesians 3:13(CEB)

A dear friend and mentor who was a survivor of the brutal "Battle of the Bulge" as a very young Army Sergeant during World War II told me that most folks are blind or unwilling to acknowledge the "elephant in the room." Until the elephant (which is symbolic of facing one's mortality) enters their respective lives they don't truly appreciate the gift of life.

Diagnosed Disease

As our first few weeks of being husband and wife brought a sense of liberation from dependent status to mature married adult status, our relationship grew stronger. However, that nagging discomfort reappeared and was now showing signs of inflammation. The ice packs I put on the inflamed area brought no relief. So, I made an appointment with our family practitioner, Dr. Brown, about six weeks into our marriage.

Dr. Brown was probably in his early 30's at the time. I really trusted and liked him. He had a relaxed, easy-going demeanor. He was quick with a smile. Encouragement and optimism were his strongest characteristics. However, as was learned, he was perfectly professional and forthright when a problem existed. Even then, he always gave an optimistic scenario in regard to the diagnosed issue.

Upon examination, Dr. Brown informed me of the likelihood that this issue was treatable; and he prescribed some medications and scheduled a follow-up appointment in the next seven to ten days. I thought the medications were improving things. But, as a dear friend has often said, "Denial is more than just a river in India."

My follow-up visit with Dr. Brown had a different air about it. Dr. Brown was not as ebullient as normal. His voice was softer and his speech more measured. He quickly determined the medications were not resolving the cause of the problem, but merely masking the symptoms. He suggested some further testing in the next couple of days to learn more about what might be the problem. My feelings at the time were of concern, but I was confident that Dr. Brown would figure this out without impeding on my busy life and newlywed status.

The follow-up test results were revealed by Dr. Brown at my third office appointment. His mood was more serious than I had ever witnessed. He explained that he thought there was a chance the issue would resolve itself; nonetheless, he had some suspicions and suggested an appointment with a young specialist new to the area, Dr. Dan Queener. Dr. Queener had just completed his clinical fellowship at Indiana University Medical Center in Indianapolis and had set up his practice in Massillon, Ohio.

I liked Dan because he also had an easy demeanor about him. He was calming, yet straightforward. And he had this flair of eccentricity that was rather cool. Dr. Queener was definitely not your father's specialist. This was a bright and innovative young doctor who was willing to go outside the defined disease protocol. I contribute much of my cancer survival to Dr. Queener's fresh knowledge, enthusiasm for his profession, and outside-the-box approach to developing treatment strategies for a complicated disease.

Within days of meeting Dr. Queener I was on my way to the operating room in Dunlap Community Hospital, where Dan would be able to surgically diagnose my problem. The unexpected results painted the worst case scenario. I had a malignant cancer that was fast growing and, if not promptly treated, would consume my lungs, brain and entire body in a few short months leading to death.

As the words came out of his mouth, it was incredibly surreal. It was too much to grasp in a short, yet compassionate conversation. Questions swirled through my 21-year-old mind. My psyche simply would not allow my mind to fully comprehend everything that was being said. But it was quite clear; I had a malignant cancer within my body, even though it could not be felt or seen. And this was a deadly cancer that was intent on snuffing out my life as quickly as it did with Butch and Ricky.

A medical game plan for attacking and defeating the cancer was Dr. Queener's focus. I could tell he had put serious thought into the course of action that would provide the best opportunity for survival. He was compassionate, but determined to come up with a creative, innovative treatment protocol. He would tell me nearly 35 years later that, at the time, there was a 90% chance that death would come for me. He was past the emotion of telling a young adult newlywed the severity of the diagnosed disease.

Unknown to me at the time, God was truly caring for my well-being when He directed me to the professionally competent and medically brilliant, Dr. Queener. However, he would tell me years later the profound affect my undaunted Spirit to endure had on him. His was a gift of medical knowledge. Mine was of the Lord, a gift of the power of the Holy Spirit to reach beyond earthly limits. These gifts would combine so that this letter of hope and encouragement could be read by you, while you find yourself searching for strength in weakness and living in the midst of disease and distress.

Dr. Queener informed me of the aggressive growth nature of the cancer with which I had been stricken. While at Indiana University Medical Center in Indianapolis he had met and worked under a cancer research doctor by the name of Lawrence Einhorn. Dan's plan of action was to get me to IUMC as soon as possible for yet another surgery. This surgery would include extensive lymph node removal. The intent was to stop the fast growing alien cells before they got to my lungs and beyond.

Tears of Terror

I can still recall, prior to going to IUMC, sitting on our sofa in the living room of the home where we had just opened our wedding presents in front of our excited and supportive family members a mere few weeks earlier. I was now alone. I much preferred to be surrounded by gregarious family and friends. Yet here I was; my family and friends and new wife were elsewhere. Suddenly, the barrage of bad news and the reality that a deadly cancer was silently chewing away inside my young and strong body brought a moment of uncontrolled tears. With no one seemingly there for me, I wept from the very core of my heart. I agonized more deeply than I had ever experienced. I was horrified!

Perplexed, dazed, distraught... mere words cannot capture the wave of distress that washed over me. It was like that experience with Debbie in the strong ocean surf in the Bahamas. In that instance, I was in control. I had the strength and will to grab her and pull her to safety. But here I was, my arms reaching for safety in the midst of a perilous and potentially deadly situation. I sensed that this danger was far beyond my control. I wondered if the strength necessary to endure could exist within.

I would learn that controlling your circumstances in life is an unattainable pursuit. We can, and should, live a healthy lifestyle that positions us to live in wellness and good health. But sometimes we are afflicted by disease and distress simply because we are fragile and fallen creatures. We typically fool ourselves into thinking we can prevent the scourge of disease and distress in our lives. On our own accord, we think we can reach immortality. Such an attitude is a lie from the great deceiver himself, Satan.

I can't begin to number the times I was questioned about my health habits by those that inquired of my cancer status. Nearly everyone would ask if I was a smoker or engaged in another bad habit that would create this diseased state. I would chuckle to myself each time I heard this question. No, I had no destructive health habits. No cigarette smoking (except those infamous 10 Kool's without the filters). No drugs. I did consume a few beers through the years. But, for the most part, I was physically active and busily engaged in earning a living.

You see, I could sense what my cancerous condition was doing to most people. There seems to exist an innate fear of disease and distress within many of us. For some goofy reason we think, *if the catastrophic illness can be linked to the afflicted person's behavior, the questioner can walk away content that such a diagnosis could never befall him or her.* The natural reaction is to ignore the "elephant in the room." Which is to say that death and destruction will not come knocking at my door. The fact remains that death and destruction is our mutual destiny.

Malignant Maelstrom

Dr. Queener was aware that Dr. Einhorn at Indiana University Medical Center had developed a yet to be FDA approved chemotherapy protocol. This chemotherapy protocol relied heavily on a newly discovered drug called Cisplatin. The treatment plan would also include other chemotherapy drugs such as Adriamycin, Bleomycin, and one yet-to-be-named drug they called VP-16.

This protocol was so cutting-edge that the treatment was unique to Dr. Einhorn's brilliant and world renowned research team at IUMC. Not even the world famous Cleveland Clinic, which was just over an hour from us, could offer this medical cocktail that gave the opportunity for a cure. The outlook for those not receiving this chemotherapy regimen was a three to six month life-span.

In looking back, it is simply unbelievable how the hand of God was working to guide and direct me to safety. There was a hand of help to which I could securely grip. It was the strong arm of the Lord who never allows his own to be snatched out of His hand. I have come to understand that in physical healing or death, it's not a matter of the fight for life in the individual; rather, it's whether Jesus Christ is engaged in the battle for life.

The truth is that Jesus Christ is an eternal healer. Whereas, healing by men, even brilliant men like Larry Einhorn, is merely a temporary healing. There are no losers in the battle with cancer when Jesus Christ is living in the midst of it all. Christ so cares for you and me that, when we cast our every care upon Him,

He provides strength through weakness... more than we could ever ask, think, or imagine. This is, was, and will forever be the sure and everlasting path to survival, while living in the midst of catastrophic disease and distress.

Greg, third grade

Gerry, Larry, Greg, Jennifer, Eloise, Doug Becker 1974

Greg and Debbie, senior prom 1975

Greg, senior picture 1975

Debbie and Greg, October 7, 1978

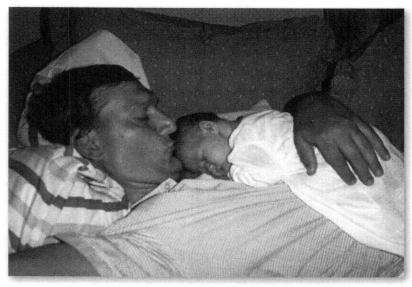

Greg and baby Katelyn

Greg and Katelyn

Greg and his girls, Kelsey and Katelyn

Greg and Kelsey

Greg and Debbie under the mistletoe

Greg and Debbie, celebrating their 25th anniversary with Kelsey and Katelyn

Greg showing off his Best Father Oscar

Nate, Katelyn, Debbie, Kelsey, Greg, Mother's Day

Katelyn and Nate's wedding, June 11, 2011

Dear lifelong friends at the wedding

Greg and Kelsey, Sunday best

Greg and Debbie

Pastor Greg

Greg and Nate, ready to kayak in Michigan, 2012

Greg's 56th birthday, January 27, 2013

Chapter 7
Confidence in the Midst

So we are always confident, because we know that while we are living in the body, we are away from our home with the Lord. 2 Corinthians 5:6 (CEB)

Within my spirit, a confident Hope had been placed. This Hope was grounded in the victory of Christ over death at Calvary. The manifestation of the chemotherapy treatments brought untold side effects requiring strength in the midst of weakness. The cancer would not succumb. Twice, the dreaded disease would re-appear claiming more territory as it worked through its destructive intentions.

Destined for Victory

That first drive out to IUMC included Debbie and I, my parents, and Debbie's parents. It was a unique trip, as we stopped along the way to eat at little restaurants that featured down-home cooking. It felt like the beginning to a family vacation. However, as we got closer to the conclusion of our five-hour trek to Indianapolis, the mood became increasingly somber. The anticipation of the unknown that awaited us in this big Midwestern city filled our hearts and minds with a wide range of emotions.

In the heart of Indianapolis, we found the Indiana University Medical Center. The facility was massive. It seemed to fill up a full city block or more. We followed the signs and ultimately found our way to Dr. Einhorn's designated section of the hospital.

The greeting by the nurses and staff was gracious and comforting. I would come to experience and admire the special gifts of the medical professionals in the IUMC oncology unit. In spite of my strengthening faith, the physical reality of the disease did not take long to manifest itself. Upon arriving at IUMC, the news got worse. The cancer was through my lymph nodes and had begun to eat away at my right lung. It was the strangest sensation to trust the words that were being said by Dr. Einhorn and his army of white-coated research doctors. His team of cancer specialists was seemingly at my bedside constantly, studying my medical chart, rubbing their chins in thought, and examining me. This brought more confidence that the challenges were being confronted with much thought. Furthermore, the challenge of contending with cancer treatments was being spiritually battled by a large group of prayer warriors.

Dr. Einhorn and his team decided they would need to take immediate action to eradicate the cancerous cells. He confidently informed me of their plan of action. Since the cancer had grown into a nodule in the lower section of my right lung, they would commence the Einhorn chemotherapy regimen. He explained that their success rate put me at a 98% chance of survival. I thought, surely, these four weeks of week-long, in-patient chemotherapy sessions could be endured. Each week of therapy would be separated by two weeks of rest and recuperation.

Chemotherapy Commences

The in-patient chemotherapy process required a 24-hour intravenous needle in the arm that would pump fluids through my body to allow the chemotherapy drugs to destroy the cancer cells, while protecting the vital organs in my body. Dr. Queener would tell me many years later that this treatment plan would one day be considered truly barbaric.

But it was, and is, the typically prescribed method for killing such a dreadful disease as cancer. The fundamentals of the science, in layman's terms, are to poison the body with the chemo drugs. The cancer cells were especially vulnerable because of the ferocity of their attack on the body. It was explained to me that this aggressive nature of my cancer made it far more deadly than most, yet much more vulnerable to destruction for the same reason. So the theory was, and is, to poison and kill the aggressive, abnormal cancer cells, as the drugs are consumed by the cancer. Meanwhile, the challenge is to protect and maintain life in the non-cancerous cells and the patient overall.

As Dr. Queener had said as he neared early retirement, I too believe that the day of modern medical technology will look back in disbelief at the brutality of the treatment of chemotherapy in the battle with cancer. I empathize in a very profound sense with you, or your loved one, as you endure cancer treatments. Thankfully, new drugs are now available that relieve many of the difficult symptoms we endured as patients in the late 70's, and work wonderfully to protect your body while undergoing chemotherapy treatments. So, don't allow the fear of chemotherapy to become the focus of your battle. Many have gone before you and endured side effects in order to find treatments that diminish those side effects.

Our mind can only be prepared for the battle with disease and distress when our heart has been supernaturally prepared. I can't emphasize enough that through my lifetime of dealing with catastrophic illness, there is an ingredient that must exist in order to persevere. The resolve, which I found to provide strength in weakness while living in the midst of a medical trauma, hinges on the existence of a supernatural transformation that must take place within the heart and soul of the afflicted.

That first day of chemotherapy treatments would be the start of a battle that would last much longer than imagined. In fact, the repercussions continue to this day, some 34 years later. The drugs were administered through the intravenous needle in my vein. As the chemotherapy entered my system, an odd sensation of a metallic nature came to the taste buds in my mouth. The drugs would take approximately forty-five minutes to drain from the hanging bags of toxic liquid into my body.

Unfortunately, I have to tell you, dear reader, that my physical reaction to the chemotherapy cocktail was quite violent. Within an hour or so I began to vomit. We counted the vomiting sessions which would include 17 episodes in the hours after receiving the treatment. After the first few, my stomach was empty and only stomach fluids would come up thereafter. My dear newlywed wife was nearby, lovingly placing what we called the "puke bucket" under my chin as another wave of nausea overcame my body. My advice is to forgo the tidy little container most hospitals use and ask for the biggest "puke bucket" they have on hand. No reason to try to be prim and proper while in the midst of uncontrolled chemotherapy-induced nausea.

Fortunately, in the days that followed, the nausea would gradually diminish, but every session brought the same reaction. It was just a matter of how many vomiting episodes would take place. I did participate in a trial that tested the impact of THC (the key ingredient in marijuana) because they theorized it might reduce the nausea caused by the chemotherapy. Because it was a trial, half of the participants received the THC and the other half received a placebo (which was simply a pill of no effect). I'm sure I got the placebo. If not, I can say from personal experience that THC had no demonstrable benefit in my case.

The first week of chemotherapy concluded and I was relieved to be on I-70 headed for home. The two weeks at home would be a welcome time of recuperation, both physically and emotionally. I don't recall much from those first four week-long treatments. My lack of recollection is probably my mind's way of coping with the trauma. There were uncomfortable side effects such as constipation, mouth sores, and shingles. My favorite snack became ice cold popsicles that were easy on the inside of my raw throat and mouth. It's a gift of the Lord that the memory of pain drifts away with time.

The Cancer Does Not Succumb

Getting through the chemotherapy regimen was a welcome relief. The spring of 1979 was sure to lead to a wonderful summer as we reconvened life out from under the storm of cancer. I was scheduled for monthly chest x-rays as a follow up to my treatment. A quiet concern was deep inside my heart, in spite of Dr. Einhorn's confident pronouncement of a 98% chance for survival.

The first chest x-ray showed that there was no sign of the cancer. It was a great relief that I had made it through the first follow-up testing and exam. After departing Dr. Queener's contemporary designed office, I let out a breath of relief. Maybe I should have had more confidence in Dr. Einhorn's prediction.

The following month I was driving to Dr. Queener's office to have another monthly exam and chest x-ray. During that drive, it occurred to me that everything that surrounded me seemed as it should be. My mind was leaving behind the ominous and ever-present cloud of cancer. But, I imagined if the cancer had returned that this news would cast an entirely different perspective on the beautiful late spring day. After all, there were no visible signs or feelings when the cancer was alive in me.

Dan invited me into his personal office, not an examining room. He had my x-ray results in front of him on the desk. He looked up at me with a look of sympathy ... IT'S BACK!

Anything else he said was mere babble. In a roar of anger I stood up, ferociously stared at my perfectly innocent doctor, threw aside my chair, ripped my wig off my head, and spiked it on his desk. I screamed out, "NO! You guys said I had a 98% chance to be healed! This is not fair. I did my part. I endured the brutal chemo. Now it's time for me to return to my carefree life as a 22-year-old." Dan assured me we had options. But I wasn't of the mindset to listen to more potentially broken promises.

I got out of his office as soon as possible and raced up the road to look for Pastor Hudson at Calvary Chapel. It was lunch time and the church sat silent and empty. A drowning wave of abandonment washed over me and swept away my emotions. I was stunned beyond tears. I was angry with God. Why, how, where, when, who are you to allow this to happen to me!?

It was not long until the embarrassment of my tirade set in. This wasn't a football game where I could physically hit and overrun my opponent. This competitor was quietly, viciously mauling me from the inside. It was winning; I was losing. I simply could not lose. The bountiful life I had imagined with my amazing wife, a successful career, wonderful kids, and all kinds of tangible and fun stuff awaited.

So, I composed myself and soon learned through Dr. Queener and Dr. Einhorn about the plan of attack. Not surprisingly, more chemotherapy would be part of the plan. This time, treatment would be comprised of two week-long sessions. However, that nodule in the right lower lobe of my lung had grown back and would need to be surgically removed first. In a very short period of time I was in the surgical waiting area of IUMC.

I was already partially sedated as they wheeled me into the first big-city hospital operating room that I had ever witnessed. It was somewhat cold, distinctly white, and comprised of stainless steel and hard surfaces. A giant light hung over a small black, thinly padded table that would serve as the operating table. The half dozen people in the room wore green masks and scrubs. They spoke in a hushed purposeful cadence. They were all business. When they addressed me, they called me "Mr. Becker," proceeded to calmly explain each step of the surgery, and encouraged me to ask any questions that came to mind.

The time had come to move me onto the operating table. The team effortlessly slid me from the gurney on which I had been transported, to the operating table and positioned me where I was comfortable and aligned with the operating room light. As the medical team prepared me, they were highly professional, competent in their task, calmly instructive, and comforting. The anesthesiologist put the intravenous needle into the vein in my right arm and said that I would sense a rush of comfort and relaxation. Soon I felt a wave of relaxation overcome my mind and body. As he administered the anesthesia for surgery, he asked that I count backward from ten. I mumbled, "ten, nine..." I don't recall anything about the surgery beyond that.

As the impact of anesthesia subsided, my eyes opened and I momentarily was confused as to where I was. What had happened? As the cobwebs of my mind cleared, I began to remember. Seemingly just a second ago I was counting down from ten, and eight was next.

Just about then, a nurse softly called my name. She methodically began to inform me that I had done well in surgery and that we were in the recovery room. The process of awakening from the anesthesia began; we would just take our time and see when I was recovered. Meanwhile, she said to rest and relax.

The fog of anesthesia began to clear and the realization of my circumstances revealed that there were a few tubes, kind of like little plastic garden hoses, that were in my right side. The nurse explained the tubes were draining unnecessary fluids from my lung. The surgeon had made a rather lengthy cut from my sternum around to my spine in order to access the lung. Dr. Queener would later say how nice and pink my lungs were, once they opened me up and cut the cancerous nodule from the right lower lobe of the lung. I am forever grateful that I had not allowed my brush with cigarette smoking to develop into an addiction that would have damaged my lungs.

A couple days later, the first of the two week-long chemotherapy treatments began. It was a bit tougher going through the nausea due to the drain tubes in my side. Plus, I didn't have the resilience as this round of chemotherapy began. I was both physically and emotionally stronger at the beginning of the first round of chemotherapy treatments.

Nonetheless we endured and, after the last treatment, Dr. Einhorn and his team remained very optimistic. I did too, surmising that by cutting the cancer nodule out of my lung and enduring a total of six week-long chemotherapy treatments, we were on the right path toward winning this cancer battle.

My memory begins to fail me in recollecting specifics of the final months of 1978 and through January, 1980. What I do recall is a brief time of thinking that I might have escaped this cell-consuming body-invader called cancer.

But, the follow up exams went the same way as before. The second monthly exam revealed the re-growth of the cancer within my right lung. A memorable conversation with the always confident Dr. Einhorn took on a much different tone. Rather than a 98% survival rate, he said our odds had slipped to 50/50. I speculated he was being optimistic.

Another surgery was scheduled, this time to remove the entire lower right lobe of my lung, in an effort to permanently eradicate the recurring cancerous disease. Four more week-long chemotherapy sessions were planned. This would be like throwing the proverbial kitchen sink at this monstrous organ-consuming curse. I was physically shrunken to a ridiculous state, hairless, muscles atrophied, emotionally dazed, a mess of a human being. Fewer friends and visitors were coming by at this point. Not hard to conclude that the aroma of death could be sensed when in my presence.

The results of the second lung surgery were seemingly dreadful. The cancer was aggressively advancing, having consumed more of my right lung and jumping over to attack my esophagus. The surgeons thought they were successful in cutting all of the cancer out of my lung and esophagus. As before, the chemotherapy commenced, while the recovery from this second lung surgery was ongoing.

Encouragers' Comfort and Direction

Throughout my cancer journey I grew close to others who were also engaged in their respective battles with this dreadful disease. Most have died and gone home to reign eternally with the Lord. One of those friends was Helen Leffler, a 50-some year-old lady of grace that was among that small Bible study group in Jack and Elaine Robinson's living room that birthed Calvary Chapel.

Helen was battling breast cancer at the same time I was engaged in my own cancer battle. Her body would succumb to the deleterious effects of breast cancer; however, her resolute faith and confidence in the hope of Christ armed her well for the battle at hand. Her effervescent smile and encouragement in the midst of disease and distress was the legacy she gave to me and so many others. She was a great and faithful inspiration to everyone that knew her.

In Helen, I would see and learn a key characteristic of those who are true warriors and champions when afflicted. Helen was always focused and earnestly praying for others, rather than wallowing in self-pity. In my lifetime, I have witnessed far too many folks that are self-focused in all realms of life. They seem impotent when facing difficult trials that require physical, emotional, and spiritual strength. They have failed to build a secure foundation. This attempt at a foundation of personal resolve without spiritual strength leaves the afflicted weak and vulnerable. We cannot escape the inevitable storm clouds that gather on the horizon and come crashing on the shores of our life. Yet, too often, a failed response is the result while living in the midst of the valleys of life.

The other encounter, which profoundly affected me, was during one of my hospital stays at Indiana University Medical Center. My roommate was a kind and gregarious African American gentleman who was in his 40's. His name was Bob Turner. He was also in the clutches of cancer.

Bob's pastor and a few of his elders stopped in the hospital room that we shared. They had come to pray for Bob and serve him communion. My Dad was in the room and they invited us both to take communion with them. It was the most intimate and powerful time of communion I would experience. It was even sweeter to share the experience with Dad. In the midst of disease and distress, the color of your skin does not divide.

Not long thereafter, they had moved Bob to a private room because death was on the doorstep. Dad and I went down the hall of the cancer unit at IUMC to visit and pray with Bob. His body had filled with fluids. He could not speak. Nonetheless, we prayed for our new friend in Christ. Bob died within days. Disease and distress are equal opportunity killers.

My second lung surgery was performed back home at Massillon Community Hospital. Dr. Einhorn's chemotherapy protocol had received FDA approval which allowed Dr. Queener to oversee this series of chemotherapy treatments and whatever else would be necessary. This created a very close doctor-patient relationship between me and Dan.

Because my cancer case was one of the first and most severe that he had encountered in his early years of private practice, I suspect he took a special interest in my case. I got the very clear impression that Dan had what I call "skin in the game." I am of the opinion that we need professional advocates like Dan who go beyond the rudimentary process of administering treatment plans, while keeping a safe emotional distance from the diseased and distressed. It is a tremendous assurance and confidence boost when we know our medical caretakers are intimately involved and concerned for our well-being.

With every ounce of physical and emotional resolve battle weary and nearly gone, my heart, mind, and spirit began a transformation that was the turning point in my cancer battle. I had fought with what I thought to be great ferocity and courage. But, the Lord wanted more of me. He no doubt patiently listened to my pleas to just live to the age of 25. He would graciously answer my desperate prayers. After all, I am now 55! An old guy, who now thinks about getting an RV rather than a muscle car.

This faith journey had taught me about the power of prayer and I had prayed many times regarding my personal condition and that of many others. Furthermore, many prayers from friends, relatives, and strangers were holding me up through what could only be described as supernatural strength. Yes, I thoroughly and completely believe that prayers in the name of our great intercessor, the Lord Jesus Christ, are of tremendous effect. The need for a supernatural power became my final and, ultimately, life-saving weapon in battling this increasingly devastating disease.

Just prior to my final chemotherapy treatment, my dear Aunt Elaine gave Debbie and Mom a break from the round-the-clock support they were providing. Never ignore the devastating impact on the loving care-keepers of those that are critically ill. Both Debbie and Mom needed some rest, both physically and emotionally, from this roller coaster ride of emotions.

Aunt Elaine, Mom's older sister and driving force behind the establishment of Calvary Chapel, stayed by my bedside through the day and into the night. I was physically spent and would often sleep and try to rally my resolve to endure yet another administration of the metallic tasting chemotherapy that invariably led to yet another session of nausea.

Aunt Elaine sat quietly by my side. She had lived a life-time, enduring her own chronic illness.

She did not force the conversation on a menial topic like the weather, the food, or some other pointless subject to simply fill the silent void with sound. She knew, by experience, the power of silence and solitude in the healing process. Because I had always admired her strong constitution, I started to ask her questions that I would never think to ask Debbie or Mom. I sensed it would be much too harsh to add that emotional burden on their already breaking hearts. They were fighting so hard so that I could live. I didn't want to disappoint them by asking a question that might indicate that my will to live was nearing the end. So, I asked Aunt Elaine the question that was heavy on my heart, "Are you prepared to die?"

She was not the least bit shaken by my question. She didn't conclude that I was giving up in my struggle to overcome cancer. Rather, I could see by her reaction that she knew I was asking for her personal approach when looking into the face of death. I was seeking assurance that I could handle the physical hardship of dying. More importantly, I wanted to hear from the depths of her heart if she believed that our mutual faith was big enough to take us all the way through death and into eternal life with Jesus Christ.

She responded compassionately in a strong and confident voice that without question she had an unshakable faith in Jesus, the God of salvation, who never lies. Our faith assures us that Christ has promised everlasting life to those who believe in Him. I could see in her eyes and hear in her voice the confident strength she had in her faith in Christ. It is not enough to know our faith intellectually. We must be able to sense and feel the deep love that we have in our relationship with Christ.

During this hospital stay, a real blessing came from the very flexible and patient-focused staff at Massillon Community Hospital. They devised an alternative plan when administering the chemotherapy. No doubt Dr. Queener was behind the unique course of action. Dan had already begun an unconventional medical trial, which included a powerful vitamin cocktail. This worked to keep the good cells in my body alive and vibrant, while the poisonous chemotherapy destroyed the radical cancer cells.

The blessing was that a member of the nursing staff sat next to my bed throughout the administration of the treatments. Just as importantly, they decided to start the treatments at night, when my body would naturally be more at rest. This approach was a stroke of genius. Apparently, the anxiety of the mid-day hours, when the treatment was normally administered, was at the time the body was most awake and alert. Thus, the repercussions created intense side effects. When administered in the evening, my body was calmer and the reaction to the drugs was greatly diminished.

Submitting and Resting

And so, after my conversation with Aunt Elaine, I was eventually alone once again. The hour was late, the room silent and dark. The hospital hallway that was normally bustling had turned calm. As I had begun to make a habit, I was praying. But this time my own voice broke the silence and I found myself praying out loud. I can recall the words as if they just came out of my mouth seconds ago. With tears in my eyes and a tremble in my voice I said, "I give up." I went on to say in my prayer: "I have nothing left. Take me or heal me. I am done."

I was thoroughly exhausted and helpless to help myself. My once strong body, in which I had taken such great pride, had been whittled from more than two hundred pounds to a skeletal-like 135 pounds. New Year's Eve of 1979 had just passed. It was almost February. Every day, I would sense that the next might not be. Yet, if I could just hold on until the first of February, my 10th week-long course of scheduled chemotherapy would mercifully come to a conclusion.

In church world, we hear talk of submitting and resting in the Lord. I found myself doing these exact things. I had submitted. I submitted what I feared most to submit, my physical life. In just over a year I was thoroughly defeated in and of my own power. I had no strength, emotions, or even prayers to speak. I allowed myself to fall into the only true and comfortable rest that I have experienced. That is to rest in the arms of a loving God. All was silent and dark once more. Strength through weakness would require a grace that was sufficient. I closed my eyes and waited.

Chapter 8
Life After Cancer

You have seen me experience physical abuse and ordeals in places such as Antioch, Iconium, and Lystra. I put up with all sorts of abuse, and the Lord rescued me from it all! 2 Timothy 3:11(CEB)

The term "cancer survivor" strikes me as an oxymoron. No one really survives this dread disease. Even when declared cured or in remission, the scars mark our body, soul, and psyche for the rest of our lives on earth. Along my path, far too many honorable and Godly people have succumbed to this dreadful disease. I ask myself, "Do they deserve to be labeled anything less than a survivor themselves?" I think not. It irritates me to no end to read or hear that someone has, "lost their battle with cancer." Hogwash; there are no losers in this battle, and I am repulsed by such language. Nonetheless, mysteriously some have been granted extended life beyond cancer and others have not. This will surely be one of the first questions I ask Jesus Christ upon entering heaven … "Why did you take them and not me?"

Walking Away From Cancer

In early February 1980, I walked out the door of Massillon Hospital not knowing what the future held. I had just celebrated my birthday in the hospital on January 27th, in the midst of the last round of chemotherapy. I was 23 years of age.

The local radio station in Wooster had allowed me to continue to work there part-time throughout my battle with cancer. I look back and think what a gracious thing that was for the management of WWST Wooster to do for me. I would work the evening shift, 5 p.m. to midnight. WWST AM would go off the air as soon as the sun set. However, WWST FM would stay on the air until midnight. Except for the national and local news at the top of the hour, the FM programming was fully automated as huge reels of tape would play easy listening music. A carousel loaded with recording cartridges that played commercials were programmed to be aired periodically.

Most summer evenings, WWST FM aired the Cleveland Indians professional baseball games. It was my duty to play the recorded commercials between innings. At the end of an inning, I would push the green button on the cartridge machine to play the 60 second commercial.

One memorable night, while engineering an Indians game, I was feeling the side effects of the chemotherapy. I was hurting, exhausted, and alone in the radio station on the top of Hillcrest Drive. Rather than remain in the control room to sit and listen to the game while awaiting the end of the inning, I was laying curled up on the couch. This old leather two-person sofa with chrome arm rests was in the lobby of the radio station, and I was listening for my cue. It was just a short walk away from the control room, and I was awaiting the third out that would conclude the inning.

To my surprise, a little old man shuffled into the radio station lobby, which also housed the Associated Press news machine from which the news of the minute would be dispensed. The machine was the radio station's link to the national and international news and provided the content of much of the information we disseminated. No, there was no world wide web to access the information we desired at any moment. It's incredible to imagine the changes that have taken place technologically since those early days of my childhood.

But, this was no ordinary old man. It was Mr. Victor Dix, the man everyone knew as the owner and publisher of The Dix Enterprises. He owned the local newspaper and others. He owned and built WWST in 1947. Mr. Dix also owned a handful of other radio stations. And there I was curled up on the old lobby sofa taking what probably appeared to be a lazy nap while on duty.

Mr. Dix did not say a thing to me. He shuffled over to the Associated Press ticker and started reading the information that was spewing out of the machine. I tried to explain my circumstances, but I am not sure he heard my words. I hustled back into the control room. Mr. Dix left without saying a word to me. I hoped I would not be fired.

To my everlasting appreciation, I was not fired. In fact, the gracious general manager, Ken Nemeth, asked me to move into a full time position with the radio station. He asked me to be their "Mobile News Reporter." This meant I would search out news stories throughout the listening area and write, produce, and record two to three minute segments that aired five times a day. My dream of being an announcer on the air had come true. Maybe luck, in regard to my health, would be the same.

For some reason, old fashioned luck, the effectiveness of the surgery and chemotherapy, the prayers and petitions that were lifted up to a merciful God; I just don't know, but it was obvious that my Creator was not done using the gifts He had given to me.

I could continue to be his instrument of faith. It is now nearly 35 years that I have survived what was a deadly cancer. How do I comprehend such a thing, when many stronger and more faithful people I met along the way ultimately succumbed physically in their cancer battle? It made no sense to me then; it makes no sense to me now. But, as long as God grants me today, I will seize it for His glory!

Home and Recreation

Life continued post-cancer. Debbie and I built a new ranch home several years later. The lot was carved from the home farm of my friend Dennis Kountz. It was a big lot that we had invested much time and energy transforming into a home. In the back of the house, a ravine provided a scenic view. A large deck overlooked the ravine and tall trees. We had old barn stones stacked on one another to create a beautiful planting area for evergreen trees and flowers. We had stained all of the exterior wood ourselves. A friend had built the house based on our design. It was a wonderful home just outside of Wooster, Ohio.

Eventually, the post-cancer future would be filled with more devastating and life threatening illness. The apparent long-term side effects of the chemotherapy that saved my life would begin to threaten my life. Until then, we enjoyed twelve years of life free of medical worries.

Another team endeavor became an opportunity to connect with good friends to achieve a seemingly impossible dream. Many Friday nights were spent playing the game of golf in the Riceland Golf Course Industrial League. Golf became an outlet for competition without the dangers of a violent sport, such as football. I certainly was nothing more than an unconventional left-handed golfer, individually. However, it was as a member of a team that I again found the opportunity to flourish.

A local tournament called the Oldsmobile Golf Scramble was first held at Riceland Golf Course in late summer and fall of 1989. A scramble tournament format requires that each of the four team members hit from the tee to start the hole. Then the best of the four shots is selected and everyone on the team moves their initial ball to the location of the best hit ball. Each team member then proceeds to hit the second shot for the scramble team from that spot. The objective is to garner the lowest score possible on each hole and ultimately the total of eighteen holes.

Our team was comprised of teammates Ken Kohlmyer, Steve Pesho, Billy Planisek, and substitute Mike Jensen, the best man in mine and Debbie's wedding. We played in what was called the handicap tournament, which meant each individual's golf handicap was incorporated into the scoring. To our surprise and delight, our total score qualified us in that local Oldsmobile Scramble golf tournament against 30 or so scramble teams, to move on to regionals in what was a national tournament.

A further bonus of qualifying for regional competition was a local club PGA professional by the name of Danny Simmons joined our scramble team. The participants in this next tournament round were the winners and qualifiers from local Oldsmobile Scramble tournaments from the Northeast Ohio region. Yet again, we found our five-man scramble team to be on top of that regional tournament, which qualified us to be one of about one hundred Oldsmobile Scramble teams that were invited to play in the National Oldsmobile Scramble tournament in Orlando, Florida. This tournament was held at Greg Norman's signature golf course, now called the International Course at Champions Gate.

Our team got off to a solid start in the national four-day golf tournament in which each scramble team played 18 holes of golf. After the third day of play, the field was cut down to the top 24 teams and a PGA professional joined each of the remaining teams. A professional golfer by the name of Robin Freeman was made the sixth member of our scramble team for that final round. We entered the final round in first place. We would conclude our unbelievable golf journey a mere stroke shy of winning the Oldsmobile Scramble National Golf Tournament. An additional highlight was that NBC television was providing highlights that later aired during the PGA Oldsmobile Golf tournament at Disney World. Imagine, our back-country scramble team of golfing buddies on national television!

To our astonishment, we would do much the same in 1990 when our team would again come up just short of winning the Oldsmobile Scramble National Tournament which was held that year at the Disney World golf courses. This time, local club PGA professional and Riceland Golf Course owner Larry Lisic became part of our regional and national qualifying scramble team. In 1990, we ended up in the third spot from among all scramble teams throughout the nation. This was truly an unexpected achievement which we were each blessed to be a part of.

Debbie and I would ultimately make our permanent family home at Lake Harmony, a recreational lake community just outside the village of Dalton, Ohio. The community was the brain-child of some area folks that wanted to build a family-oriented lake community in the 1960's. The men were devout Christians and had done well financially.

They bought a farm and carved out a lake big enough for boating and water skiing at the lowest point of the property. This lake has a distinctive island in the middle of it. Our family would drive by Lake Harmony as we headed east on State Route 30 on our trek from Apple Creek to church in Massillon throughout my childhood and into adulthood.

Lake Harmony has approximately 90 lots about an acre each. In the 1960's, we thought of the neighborhood and homes as opulent. Today, they are simply solid middle-class homes. We live in a spacious white ranch that we bought from one of the founders of Lake Harmony when our youngest daughter, Kelsey, was just one year old. It has been my occasion to serve on the community board of Lake Harmony, which serves to utilize the property assessments to maintain and enhance the common areas which the community can access.

We have lake beaches on the north and south ends. Picnic pavilions and open spaces to run, walk, and enjoy the outdoors are also available. We host at least two family reunions here at Lake Harmony each year. This past summer, we welcomed our Calvary Chapel church family, as well, for a picnic, swimming, and boating. We are surrounded by the best neighbors you could imagine. They include a pastor, an engineer that graciously assists far beyond the call, and my cardiologist and friend who is two doors away.

Chapter 9
In Sickness and Health

Let my enemy not only chase but catch me trampling my life into the ground, laying my reputation in the dirt. Psalm 7:5 (CEB)

As we stand before God and the gathered witnesses to exchange our wedding vows, we commit to one another to stick to our nuptials through sickness and health. My battles with difficult medical complications had only begun with cancer. In subsequent years, Debbie would be by my side through heart failure, respiratory failure, complicated open heart surgery, kidney failure, and daily dialysis. Her unwavering faithfulness would testify to her love for the Lord and the presence of the Holy Spirit within her soul.

Cardiomyopathy

During the spring of 1990, I was raking leaves and gathering tree limbs in the ravine behind our house. For some reason, I realized that I was very winded, unlike I had ever been before. I had been dealing with chest congestion for a while. I also had noticed that my ankles were uncharacteristically swollen on occasion. I didn't quite understand what was up with me.

But I was busy working and doing my chores around the house. My Grandma Becker had passed away rather suddenly, which further distracted me from these physical issues. These problems were causing an increasing amount of fluid in my lungs and ankles. I recall going to Grandma's funeral service with ankles that made it difficult to put on my shoes.

My dentist and longtime mentor from Calvary Chapel, Dr. David Leffler, took note of my swollen ankles and strongly encouraged me to have them checked out with the doctor immediately. I did, and I soon found myself in the cardiology department at the Cleveland Clinic. I had won a business trip at work to the sunny southwest United States due to a very good year of sales production, so I didn't have much time for this visit to the Cleveland Clinic. After cardiologist Dr. Bott-Silverman examined me, she told me I would be admitted immediately. I was in heart failure. There would be no vacation and frivolity in the sun with my accomplished cohorts.

It would not be long until I learned of the severity of my condition. I had a heart virus that had terribly weakened my heart. The heart muscle was simply not squeezing enough to push the life-saving blood throughout my body. Again, as if it were yesterday, I recall Dr. Bott-Silverman pulling back the curtain that hid my roommate from view. She introduced me to Eustice, a genteel African American man. Eustice was there for his one year check up on his heart transplant. Dr. Bott-Silverman told me I would more than likely need the same. I gulped.

Upon seeing Eustice, a broad smile came across his face and he introduced himself in a very jovial, yet serious manner. In a matter-of-fact tone, Eustice said to stop messing around with the consequences of heart failure and go for the transplant. Yikes! I admired him; but, I wasn't too keen on the whole idea. I had grown rather fond of the heart in my own chest cavity.

There was a 40% chance, according to the Cleveland Clinic heart team, that my heart muscle would improve so that I could escape the need for such a huge surgery at the age of 33. I prayed for the heart muscle to restore itself. Amazingly, it did. Who can imagine such a blessing? It was certainly beyond my expectation. However, the long-term repercussion of this viral myocarditis was diminished kidney function, as well as a permanent amount of heart failure.

Respiratory Distress

Prior to the next medical event that would take us down a road of life-challenging consequences, I had a heart attack while in my mid 30's. A clearing of the occluded artery in my heart would be performed.

Then in late 1999, on the verge of the change of the millennium, I was scheduled for what was expected to be an easy gall bladder surgery at Dunlap Hospital in Orrville. By now, you probably have guessed this was not an "easy" surgery. Seems that is the way things have been for me.

The morning after the gall bladder surgery, Dr. Brown stopped into my room to check on my progress. Uncharacteristically, I could tell that I was having great difficulty breathing. Dr. Brown had entered my room ever-cheerful, as always. However, he quickly took note of my distress. He immediately realized my blood oxygen level had plummeted to extremely low levels. I was virtually drowning in my own bodily fluids that were building up in my lungs.

The new cardiologist in town came into my room. His name was Dr. George Seese. Most friends called him, "Skip." Dr. Seese hustled to prepare me to be transferred to a larger hospital in

Canton, Ohio. Aultman Hospital was about a half-hour away. That half-hour trip was much shorter as the ambulance driver pushed the truck engine to its maximum. We roared south out of the small town hospital, made a hard left turn to the east at Riceland Golf Course, and high tailed it across State Route 30 toward Aultman Hospital. Even in my distress, I could sense that the driver was negotiating the 20 minute drive as quickly and safely as possible. We flew by our home at Lake Harmony with Dr. Seese in close pursuit in his own vehicle.

Upon arrival at the Aultman Emergency ambulance entrance, the paramedics whisked me into the hospital. I could sense I was on the verge of passing out. From that point on, I would learn of what would happen second-hand from my family.

It seems there was an official protocol that the nurses felt bound to follow. Skip entered the room, in which I lay laboring to breathe, and turned the place upside down. This caring, easy-going, delightful guy swore at the staff and told them to step aside and forget their over-regulated protocol. Skip would heroically save my life in the moments to come.

This was merely the beginning of yet another lengthy time of physical distress that plummeted me into the depths. I had a tracheotomy and was put on a ventilator in a state of semi-consciousness for several weeks. The team of doctors was trying to allow my lungs to fight the infection that had overwhelmed my system. They referred to my condition as sepsis.

One of the truly miraculous parts of this lengthy hospital stay was the pastoral care I received from an unexpected source. You may recall my mention of the horror on my friend's face at our wedding when we realized that our pastor was missing. This same friend was also stunned when, during a pick-up football game while being touched down, the force of the touch caused my wig to fly off my chemo-induced hairless head. The man in the midst of both these events was Randy Weaver. He was yet another dear high school friend.

To the surprise of many, Randy had recently enrolled in the Ashland Theological Seminary as an adult student after nearly twenty years working in various roles within Human Resources. He was one of the most caring and gracious guys I knew. But, to his wife's dismay, she attended church each Sunday alone. Candy recognized Randy's kind heart. Randy and Candy were also students at Waynedale High School with Debbie and I. They had started dating on the same weekend as us. It is truly incredible to look back to see how God has woven together the tapestry of what seemed to be a meaningless and randomly comprised path of life.

The Lord answered Candy's prayers when Randy went to church with her for the first time. When the long-time couple entered the sanctuary of the little Congregational Church in tiny Holmesville, Ohio, Randy sought out a spot as far away from the pulpit as he could find. He would go back the next Sunday, and then the next. Within a short period of time, this compassionate Human Resource Director, who was always known to listen to his employee's problems, found himself drawn to faith in Jesus Christ. Randy came to understand that, in Christ, he found answers to the problems of others. These solutions were far superior to mere words of concern and acts of compassion.

Subsequently, as the Lord worked on Randy's spiritual heart, he was drawn to enroll at seminary. While studying and attending seminary, Randy was pastoring two little congregations in Lakeville and Bigelow. I remember Randy standing nearby with my friends as the medical team was preparing to put me on the ventilator. That same look of concern and bewilderment that I had seen on his face on the day of our wedding was once again written all over him. Randy and these dear high school friends had somehow heard of the medical distress I was facing. They rushed over to Aultman Hospital to support Debbie and possibly encourage me by their presence. I could see my friends; but, I am not sure they could see me. The look on their faces was of profound affection and concern. Debbie and I are so blessed to have such friends.

This would not be the last visit Randy would make to the hospital on my behalf. He made the two hour round trip to see me nearly every day of many weeks I spent on the ventilator, while in a medically induced coma. Although I was unable to acknowledge his presence, I knew Randy was there. I could see his head bowed at my side, vigorously praying for me. Just think, Randy performed this ritual time after time and the patient could not respond to his presence. Randy would not be deterred in the call of ministering to his high school friend. What a guy!

The days ran together and are not remembered by me. After an extended time in this condition, the administration of steroids seemed to bring a glimpse of relief. It was enough for the medical team to wean me off the ventilator. A week later my lungs again filled with fluid and I very reluctantly allowed them to put me back on the ventilator. I pleaded with Debbie not to let them do it; so much for following the directives of the patient in the midst of disease and distress. My sweetheart for life knew I had the strength and perseverance to endure the weakness that had overcome me.

Eventually, having finally been weaned off the ventilator, my faithful friend and burgeoning pastor was again by my side. This time I could communicate with Randy. As I had done 20 years earlier with Aunt Elaine, I shared my concern that I had no strength with which to continue. There were no tears or words of distress that Randy spoke; instead, he reached into his coat pocket and pulled out a velvet wrapped bottle of oil and began to go through the spiritual preparations in silence to anoint me with the oil.

Our church did not practice such acts of worship; however, I joyously and gratefully submitted to Randy's expression of faith because I recognized his deep spiritual sincerity that was motivating him to do this on my behalf. He slowly and gently applied the oil that symbolized the atonement of Christ on my forehead. I was immediately comforted and spiritually moved. Randy then prayed aloud that the Master Healer would touch my broken body and restore my health. Sincerity in Christ brings salt to the earth. Salt is a preserving agent that brings healing and sweetness to those on which it is sprinkled.

Within two weeks, I was home with my family. Our girls were eleven and seven years of age. I was motivated not to leave Debbie a young widow and my girls fatherless at such a tender time in their respective lives. The care by my family, the Dalton school teachers, our church family, friends, and our parents while I persevered through this medical episode was overwhelming. I will forever be indebted to them all for their gracious care, concern, and love that was poured out on our little family.

Heart Surgery Complications

Seven years later, my luck would run out once again. While at our home at Lake Harmony, I was struggling with chest pain in our living room wing-back chair. As much as I hoped that it was a mere muscle pull in my chest, I finally relented late in the evening.

Debbie called the emergency squad and notified Dr. Seese who now lived two doors away from us.

Skip burst into our living room in his Pittsburgh Steelers sweats after he had run the three hundred feet from his house to ours. He looked at me with seriousness and determination in his eyes. His first question was: "What's going on Greg?" Minutes later, the EMTs arrived and Skip began to bark out orders to them. The surprise in the EMTs' faces was rather funny in the midst of a serious situation. Who was this fellow in the Pittsburgh Steelers sweats telling them what to do? Hey, this was my good neighbor and personal cardiologist who had saved my life once, and was by my side once more while in the midst of cardiac distress.

They quickly packed me in the ambulance as the bright red pulsating lights from the vehicle lit up our neighborhood. I would be stabilized at Dunlap Hospital personally by Dr. Seese. The emergency room nurses cut my clothes off and put me on forced oxygen while Skip worked as a maestro in the emergency room directing the nurses to administer medication and to do it quickly. It took a while, but I could feel the oxygen reaching my lungs... soon I could breathe. As soon as Skip and the medical team determined it was safe to be transported, an ambulance took me, once again, on the brisk drive east on State Route 30 to Aultman Hospital in Canton.

A heart catheterization was performed and the doctor performing the procedure stopped the test almost immediately. It was obvious within moments that I had multiple heart blockages and would need open heart surgery.

To my delight, a former business associate, Dr. Antonio Chryssos, walked into my hospital room. He was the excellent thoracic surgeon we had promoted to large employer groups while I was working for the health plan that featured Dr. Chryssos. We would regularly invite owners and management of larger companies in the area to a luncheon in the board room of the hospital. Dr. Chryssos was personally introduced to our visitors and he spoke to them of his heart program's unmitigated success and his availability. A tour of the heart center designed by Dr. Chryssos was held after this personal conversation with the well-respected thoracic surgeon.

I can remember asking one of Dr. Chryssos' nurses about what made him so special. She said it was all in his hands. She said that he had the hands of a professional pianist. Watching him do a heart procedure was like watching a virtuoso performance.

After evaluating my heart catheterization results, he spoke to me in a confident, matter of fact way. Dr. Chryssos informed me of the multiple blockages and that he was prepared to perform the necessary surgery on my heart Monday morning. I had noticed while working with him that he had, what I would describe as, a God-complex. He was so confident of his abilities and had endured most any kind of challenge while performing open heart surgery that he was confident no heart situation was beyond his ability to resolve. I like that in an open-heart surgeon.

Dr. Chryssos would bypass five of my heart arteries in a five-hour morning procedure. He had a second bypass procedure scheduled for that afternoon. As it turned out, I don't think that his afternoon surgery was performed until another day. During bypass surgery, a drug is administered to thin out the blood for easier flow during recovery. In my case, we would later learn that this drug was possibly tainted from the manufacturer. This led to further complications following the surgery.

I was sent to post-surgery recovery, which I do not remember. Within hours, Dr. Chryssos' team recognized that life-threatening internal bleeding was occurring and the team rushed me back into the operating room. He operated for a few hours trying to clean up the mess. Post-surgery, I was sent to recovery for a second time.

But the massive bleeding did not subside and, within a few hours, Dr. Chryssos was again operating on me in an attempt to save my life. The third procedure was performed and, yet again, I returned to post-operative recovery. By now, you are probably thinking my story is purely fiction. But, trust me, I have many witnesses.

This third operation within a matter of 24 hours was successful. I have no idea how Dr. Chrysoss maintained the stamina, concentration, and determination to pull me through. But, like I said, this guy had a God-complex. It was well-deserved and much appreciated by me and my family.

Kidney Failure

I had entered the surgery with diminished kidney function, as a result of the cardiomyopathy that had weakened my heart muscle back in 1990. The tremendous stress on my body from the unrelenting internal bleeding contributed significantly to the failure of my kidney function. Yet again, we were in for a prolonged hospital stay. In addition, my platelets had plummeted as a result of the blood-thinner. The infectious disease doctor said we could only wait and treat with the standard protocol to see if my platelets would recover to normal levels.

There would be no recovery for my kidneys. Soon, I was enduring my first dialysis treatment. Nothing scared me more than the thought of being on dialysis. I was petrified during that first dialysis session. The temporary port they had put in my neck seemed inadequate to hold the dialysis hook up because it kept beeping throughout. The dialysis nurse sat with me for the 4 hours of treatment and would adjust the dialysis machine and the port in my neck each time we heard the loud beep of the machine. I remained stiff as a board throughout that first treatment. I would refuse to believe my nephrologist, Dr. Kelly, when he informed me that dialysis would be a permanent part of my life from that point forward. I was sure my kidney function would return to a level adequate for this to merely be a temporary circumstance.

Five years later, I remain on peritoneal dialysis. The nightly at-home treatments last eleven hours from start to finish. The dialysis is relatively easy on my system, but the effects are undeniable. I meet with Dr. Kevin Kelley monthly to review my blood results and adjust medications. Again, I have been blessed with a great physician. Kevin is a bright, articulate, well put-together young man. I like that he was a rugged football running back in high school. He is very competitive. Much of our time during my monthly appointment is spent chatting about our families and the stuff of life. I like this guy a lot.

In the year after the beginning of dialysis, I met with the transplant teams at the Cleveland Clinic and The Ohio State Medical Center. Both determined that, in addition to a kidney transplant, I was in need of a heart transplant. My diminished lung function thwarted the idea from proceeding. In addition, the many blood transfusions that I had received over the years made organ rejection an almost certain probability. As both teams told me, a failed kidney transplant can be rectified, but a heart transplant is irrevocable. So tonight, as I write, it's time to get hooked up for my nightly eleven hours of dialysis. Good night.

Chapter 10
Perseverance

You have shown endurance and put up with a lot for my name's sake, and you haven't gotten tired. Revelation 2:3 (CEB)

Oftentimes, I believe that people live out their lives as if they have been administered anesthesia. They seemingly have no depth of feeling of euphoria or agony. My journey to find strength through weakness on the path of life has taken me through cancer and other catastrophic illnesses. Throughout, it has been apparent that we must face that which we must endure from a perspective of reality. In other words, we dare not anesthetize ourselves to the severity of the disease or distress. We must face our trials head on. We are failing ourselves and our loved ones if we don't.

Reactions: Positive

The overall outpouring of care, cards, prayers, and loving concern in the midst of my battle with cancer was far beyond my wildest expectation. The get well cards would eventually fill multiple grocery bags. I still have those cards of encouragement and prayerful concern that are now more than 34 years old tucked away in storage.

So many people of whom I have written, and those who do not appear in this book, have strengthened my will and positively impacted my life. For that I am eternally grateful. I wish that every person that has prayed, supported, and loved me and my family could be found noted in this book "Strength Through Weakness." But, more importantly, the Lord has taken note and knows the heart of every person. He will offer rewards to these dear ones beyond any I could ever dream to provide.

Reactions: Not-So-Positive

During your diseased condition, you may experience some not-so-positive and rather unexpected reactions. These unexpected reactions may be as harmless as my friend who, when reacting to my hairless head, blurted out "Greg, you look like a Martian."

I must admit the loss of my hair made me more than a bit vain. I can remember my hair filling the sink increasingly during day after day of shampooing. I voluntarily relented and took the next step. I began to painlessly pull my hair out by the handful as I stood before the mirror that morning. Remember, I was a child of the 70's. I enjoyed growing my hair long as was the style of my generation. With each fist-filled hand of my long silky hair was a real sense of my lost youth.

I would resort to wearing a full wig that I purchased from Rich the barber in Wooster. Rich was a hip, toupee'-wearing dude. For men that were going bald, Rich featured special assistance. Two engaging lady barbers were in the front of his barber shop. They cut men's hair in a free-spirited manner in traditional barber chairs. Behind the wall, Rich offered his private specialized help in a less conspicuous area. I explained my situation and he compassionately fitted me with a men's wig in the private confines of Rich's Barber Shop.

I had a number of awkward, yet hilarious, situations while wearing that wig. The funniest occurred at Randy Weaver's house, my friend who had yet to find his calling in the pastorate. We were playing a pick up football game in the side yard of his renovated two-story home. Shockingly, while I was trying to elude a defender after catching the football, the defender got hold of me and my wig flew from my bald head! Hairless as a newborn, I stood before him. What on earth had he done? Utter confusion and bewilderment was written across his face. Eventually, we were all rolling on the ground in laughter.

Blessings Born

September 20, 1988, was a bright and beautiful sunshine-splashed fall morning. We were back at Dunlap Hospital in Orrville almost 10 years after my tragic cancer diagnosis on that cloudy early November day.

This was a far more glorious scheduled appointment for surgery. Our, yet to be born, first daughter was doing what she has done for a lifetime.

In her typical strong-willed manner, our first child was doing things her own way. This meant our soon-to-be newborn was entering the birth canal from the wrong direction. Technically, she was what Dr. Brown described as "breech." She was feet-first rather than being positioned head-first as she entered the birth canal. This meant Debbie would have to deliver her by way of a Cesarean section.

On that glistening morning, it was as if all was perfect in our world. We were about to begin our longed-for family with a daughter. I was given permission to be at my high school sweetheart's side as Dr. Brown brought Katelyn into this world. As the nurse held up a screaming baby girl, our daughter was arriving with a loud pronouncement to the world! As the nurse cleaned her up, our newborn baby continued to fully utilize her little lungs. "Is she okay?" was my first reaction addressed to Dr. Brown. In his typical reassuring manner he said, "That is a healthy girl!" Oh my, what a blessing to hear those words. I was overwhelmed by this precious gift and tears filled my eyes. The Lord had answered and given us our long prayed for gift of a child. Truly, the Lord is good to those that love Him.

The nurse put our newborn, noisy daughter next to Debbie's radiant face. Debbie whispered, as this crying child was put in the arms of her loving mother, "Everything is okay, Katelyn." And thus, the life of Katelyn Elizabeth (Becker) Shultz commenced. I don't know for sure, but, more than likely, her life began in the same operating room where mine had begun a march in a much more ominous direction.

We were now a family. Katelyn's birth turned our 10 years of focusing on ourselves as a couple into a totally new dynamic. Pastor Hudson had taught parents of the "nurture and admonition of the Lord" when raising children. I was determined to raise this little girl to have a strong constitution and a heart that was of the Lord. I wanted my child to be strong, resourceful, and independent if something were to happen.

Meanwhile, I was working as an Account Executive (basically, I sold health insurance plans to employer groups) for one of the nation's largest health insurers. I had yet to finish my bachelor's degree. I knew in order for my career opportunities to be fully realized for me and my family, I would need to complete my schooling. I was about a year short of having my degree. I had allowed this non-fulfillment of a needed accomplishment to happen because of the twists and turns of cancer and my procrastination. I was putting the finishing touches on my bachelor's degree by the time Katelyn was born.

I knew it was time to get our family's spiritual house in order. So, in addition to completing my degree and remaining on a career path that provided well for my family, it was time to re-capture the faith that I had proclaimed many years earlier at Grace Youth Camp as a teenager. We decided to make Calvary Chapel in Massillon our home church after attending a few other churches prior to Katelyn's birth. The beautiful colonial style building stood on Wales and Stuhldreher on the north end of Massillon. The new Calvary Chapel facility was closer to the new neighborhoods that were being constructed as compared to the initial church building on 8th Street in downtown Massillon. I had a hand in constructing the original building in my teen years. It was, and is, a stately facility patterned in a Williamsburg style.

Those attracted to Calvary Chapel have said of our colonial-style church "it looks the way a church should look." Most importantly, the people that comprise the heart of Calvary Chapel make the ministry what a church should be. I wish every young man and woman could be touched throughout his or her life by the men and women of Calvary Chapel. For many of us, the lives of these individuals have served to nurture, admonish, encourage, and build lives that testify to the Lord Jesus Christ. The result is that many have come out of this small ministry to serve in the ministry, on the mission field, and in their work place.

The second-most exciting day of our marriage was Monday, May 18, 1992. Debbie was nine months pregnant and, the afternoon before, was awakened from a Sunday nap after church. Suddenly, without warning, her water had broken. We had sung in the Calvary Chapel choir that morning and she often thought how embarrassing this would have been had it happened just hours earlier, while standing in front of the congregation!

Not much was happening while Debbie waited in her nicely appointed maternity room at Dunlap Hospital in Orrville throughout the late afternoon and into the night of the 17th. Kelsey was being compliant as usual, and she was properly positioned for birth. We would see if Debbie could give birth naturally to Kelsey Anne as was Dr. Brown's plan.

Debbie was 35 and, even though she was in good health, her age was possibly going to make this process rather challenging. I am sure if you are a lady that has given birth to a child, you may have laughed aloud after reading that last sentence in regard to child birth being "challenging." You are right ladies, I have no idea of the pain and agony of child birth. But, I was admiringly present in the hospital room with Debbie and the medical folks awaiting Kelsey's arrival.

On the morning of the 18th, it became apparent that some help would be needed to move the process along. She was given a drug called Pitocin that would do just that. However, as is her habit, Kelsey was quite content to take it easy for a while. After all, there is no reason to rush into anything. Finally, Kelsey eased into our family late in the afternoon after lots of work on her mother's part. Debbie would say, "Now our family is complete."

Dreams Delivered

To tell of the 20 plus years of childrearing fun, adventure, and joy that grew our girls into wonderful adult ladies, of whom Debbie and I are so proud, would require volumes of books. They are our legacy to the future. I think, because we realized what a precious commodity life has been, we were able to be unique parents to the daughters God has given us.

I can't put my finger on it, but in some ways, it is my observation that many parents of today do not value their children. Oh sure, the parents of today may call their children precious; and they certainly express their love for their kids by spilling untold dollars into organized, safe, strictly structured events. The children of today play baseball, softball, volleyball, dancing, baton twirling, you name it... the game is highly organized.

There are no more pick-up games such as I benefitted from as a kid. Back in the day, we kids determined the activity, the rules of the game, the conduct that was expected. If we wanted a fancy field on which to play, we went up the street to the hardware and bought the chalk to outline the field ourselves. We did the design and organization of things, and we took pride in what we had done.

There were no regulators, and the score was kept to determine the winner. Of course, in our modern and evolved society, now we don't want to keep score. We want all participants to be treated the same. So, today the kids keep track of the score themselves while the parents tear down the scoreboards.

Unfortunately, I believe the unintended consequence is a child that grows into adulthood with no understanding as to how they are to make their way through life without someone holding their hand. Emotionally, they linger as immature children unwilling and incapable of being a responsible adult. Physically they are grown up, emotionally they remain in childhood. I have noted that this phenomenon is far too prevalent especially among our young men of today. This pattern of eternal immaturity typically leads to a failure of leadership among our men that forces many young mothers to fend for themselves.

So, I guess you can say that Debbie and I were old school parents. Not long after our family was complete, Debbie walked away from her secure and good-paying position as treasurer of the school district from which we graduated. I was the sole breadwinner, and it was my responsibility to provide. And I wanted to provide as well for my girls as was possible. Sometimes I did very well, other times not as well. But, the Lord always provided all that we needed as I negotiated the medical challenges that typically had a deleterious effect on our family income.

We were, and continue to be, fully engaged in our girls' lives. We do our best not to just talk of our love, but to demonstrate our love to them. We tried to foster a loving and affectionate bond between our daughters and ourselves as we both learned from our parents. We have found that a friend-like relationship weakens, while a mature parent/child relationship strengthens.

We dare not brag or boast about our parental expertise. I have witnessed first-hand far too many children raised by loving, well-meaning, even Christian, parents that have lost their way. Much prayer and commitment went into the parenting of our daughters, Katelyn and Kelsey. It is now their responsibility as to the course of life they choose for themselves.

We like to think our girls are doing quite well and will continue to be a blessing to the lives they touch. They will, without question, bring light into this lost and dark world. I assure you our dreams have been delivered through our little family. I believe this is because of the perspective that was impressed upon our lives as we found strength through weaknesses brought on by cancer, disease, and distress.

Unexpected Turn

Although, in retrospect, the Lord had been preparing me for over 50 years to do what He intended with my life; He then sent what I thought to be an unexpected turn in my path. I became the pastor of our beloved church, Calvary Chapel in Massillon, Ohio.

I really don't know where to begin, or how to explain this change in the course of my life. I never saw myself in such a role. I was, and am, thoroughly inadequate to fulfill the duties of pastor. Nonetheless, I have learned through this inexplicable life, "Here I am Lord... use me."

My sense of inferiority for such an undertaking is further pronounced because of the vast knowledge and academia that I saw and honored in Pastor Hudson. Yet, it was Dr. Henry T. Hudson who was adamant that I lead the flock at Calvary. As I serve as pastor to the church he founded through the grace of a giving and merciful Savior, Henry continues to be my mentor and encourager.

I would like to tell you that our 400-seat colonial style sanctuary is filled each Sunday morning that I step to the platform to preach. However, that is not the case. As has been in my physical life, my time in the pastorate has had its ups and downs. Each time I step up to the podium, I do as I learned in radio. I speak as if having a conversation with you, the individual. I don't talk to a crowd. I seek to speak one-on-one, directly to each person. The number of individuals that hear my words will ultimately be determined by the Lord.

God has taught me patience the very hard way. I choose not to view life as difficult or as if I am a victim. In fact, as I think of it, life can be quite hard if we allow it to be defined as being victimized.

When we believe in our hearts that Christ has promised to make us more than conquerors, I believe we find strength in the midst of weakness, even when disease and distress are a big part of life. Because, as the Gospel writer in Matthew has written, "God's yoke is easy," we can experience the easiness of the Comforter.

Chapter 11
Encouragement to You

Lord, you listen to the desires of those who suffer. You steady their hearts; you listen closely to them, Psalm 10:17 (CEB)

Thank you for taking this journey through my words of recollection and impressions as I persevered through the challenges of disease and distress. As you have seen through my personal narrative, there have been struggles and there have been incredible blessings. Through it all, I trust you have seen that keeping your eye focused toward eternity will guide you through the trials and tumult of today. So, I would like to conclude with this final thought of encouragement to you. You can find strength through weakness.

You Can Do This!

In writing this letter for you, I trust that you have noticed the many gifted and gracious people that a caring God has placed in my life. I do not believe these many people, of whom I have written, were haphazardly directed toward me. To get to 55 years of life and find the role for which God purposed me, I needed a lot of maturation, care, and love.

As is clear, the folks I have mentioned were "yielded and fervent" people. Yielding your life to God is not what our culture tells us to do today. Society says to never yield. As the cancer victim and inspirational college basketball coach, Jimmy Valvano, famously said while in the waning days of death by cancer: "Don't give up. Don't ever give up."

Yet I am suggesting the opposite approach based on my faith and lifetime of experience. I trust you have seen through my personal experiences that who and what you "give up" is the key to finding strength through weakness. I suggest you welcome the hope of heaven on earth and eternity with Jesus Christ rather than the weak and vacant hope that this world has to offer. I trust that you have captured the mystical power of the people of faith whose lives have intersected with mine. Scripture calls them *a "peculiar people" that have and are still seeking and trusting the pure* things of God with a great motivation to see goodness brought into this world. Titus 2:14 (KJV) *Who gave himself for us, that he might redeem us from all iniquity, and purify unto himself a **peculiar people**, zealous of good works.*

The hand of The Master Planner has unquestionably authored this story of strength through weakness. His grace has indeed been sufficient. You see, this is not my story personally. This is the story of a caring God that never fails to faithfully see us through life's every battle and blessing. He provides beyond all that we could ask or imagine. His is the strong and sure yoke that is easy for those of us that labor in the midst of heavy burdens. He has promised an abundant life when we invite Him into our lives. I trust you have seen the hand of God in this letter and not the weak and frail hand of this author.

As I end this heartfelt letter of reality and encouragement to you, I want to share my confidence in the Hope that I have attempted to convey in my personal narrative, corresponding Bible verses, practical principles, and pictures for perspective. No one's journey while seeking strength in the midst of disease and distress is the same.

So, these are simply my thoughts gleaned through the challenges I have endured and the truths I hold dear, because of my faith in the people and Word of God. Your journey may be similar or quite different from that of my own. Of this I am sure: the Wisdom of the Ages, in cooperation with the brilliance of modern science, can provide supernatural, eternal healing and temporary physical healing. An eternal perspective allows short-term survival the best chance to occur while you are found to be living in the midst.

Fear will choke out life; whereas, a confident hope in the things of God brings victory every time you invite the Lord into the fray. Never run from your troubles. Rather, turn toward them, get your head and heart right with the Omnipotent One, the all-powerful God of the universe, and sprint headlong at full speed right at those troubles. I pray that you will close the final page of this book with that eternal perspective that serves as the lasting foundation to persevere through life's greatest challenges. Please know that these words that have been written to you have been bathed in my own personal prayer, and those of the many who have been by my side and seek for you to have a personal relationship with Jesus Christ.

You are loved by this author and, more importantly, you are so loved by the author and finisher of your life, the Lord Jesus Christ. He is to be praised!

Epilogue

Greg went home to be with his Savior less than a month after completing this memoir. Consequently, he did not have time to finish this final section of biblical principles and personal reflections. We have included the principles and applicable scripture that he related to the first few chapters, and we encourage you to be a "Berean" and "search the scriptures" for verses relating to the remainder of the book. (Acts 17:10-11)

Greg's intent was to use this section of principles and scripture references as a Bible study guide, devotional, or support group outline. We pray that it points you to Jesus, the only true source of strength through weakness, and "May the God of hope fill you with all joy and peace as you trust in him, so that you may overflow with hope by the power of the Holy Spirit." (Romans 15:13)

<u>Greet Graciously</u>

> Genesis 18:2 (NIV): Abraham looked up and saw three men standing nearby. When he saw them, he hurried from the entrance of his tent to meet them and bowed low to the ground.

> Titus 3:15 (NIV): Everyone with me sends you greetings. Greet those who love us in the faith. Grace be with you all.

> 1 Thessalonians 5:26 (KJV): Greet all God's people with a holy kiss.

<u>Life Changes in an Instant</u>

> Psalm 126:4 (NIV): Restore our fortunes, Lord, like streams in the Negev.

> 2 Corinthians 7:9 (NIV): Yet now I am happy, not because you were made sorry, but because your sorrow led you to repentance. For you became sorrowful as God intended and so were not harmed in any way by us.

<u>Speak with Substance</u>

> 1 Corinthians 13:11 (NIV): When I was a child, I talked like a child, I thought like a child, I reasoned like a child. When I became a man, I put the ways of childhood behind me.

> Acts 13:46 (NIV): Then Paul and Barnabas answered them boldly: "We had to speak the word of God to you

first. Since you reject it and do not consider yourselves worthy of eternal life, we now turn to the Gentiles.

Acts 18:26 (NIV): He began to speak boldly in the synagogue. When Priscilla and Aquila heard him, they invited him to their home and explained to him the way of God more adequately.

Solitude Matures

Ecclesiastes 3:7 (NIV): a time to tear and a time to mend, a time to be silent and a time to speak,

Acts 8:32 (NIV): He was led like a sheep to the slaughter, and as a lamb before its shearer is silent, so he did not open his mouth.

Persevere Beyond Your Power

1 Timothy 4:16 (NIV): Watch your life and doctrine closely. Persevere in them, because if you do, you will save both yourself and your hearers.

1 Peter 5:10 (NIV): And the God of all grace, who called you to his eternal glory in Christ, after you have suffered a little while, will himself restore you and make you strong, firm and steadfast.

Establish Your Children

Ezekiel 16:62 (KJV): And I will establish my covenant with thee; and thou shalt know that I am the LORD:

Psalm 87:5 (NIV): Indeed, of Zion it will be said, "This one and that one were born in her, and the Most High himself will establish her."

Ephesians 6:4 (KJV): And, ye fathers, provoke not your children to wrath: but bring them up in the nurture and admonition of the Lord.

Find Friends of Faith

Ephesians 6:21 (NKJV): But that you also may know my affairs and how I am doing, Tychicus, a beloved brother and faithful minister in the Lord, will make all things known to you;

Romans 1:13 (NKJV): Now I do not want you to be unaware, brethren that I often planned to come to you (but was hindered until now), that I might have some fruit among you also, just as among the other Gentiles.

God Leads the Surrendered

2 Chronicles 30:8 (NKJV): Now do not be stiff-necked, as your fathers were, but yield yourselves to the Lord; and enter His sanctuary, which He has sanctified forever, and serve the Lord your God that the fierceness of His wrath may turn away from you.

Ephesians 5:21 (NKJV): submitting to one another in the fear of God.

Reach Out to Others

Psalm 96:2 (NKJV): Sing to the Lord, bless His name; Proclaim the good news of His salvation from day to day.

2 Corinthians 1:5 (NKJV): For as the sufferings of Christ abound in us, so our consolation also abounds through Christ.

2 Timothy 1:8 (NKJV): Therefore do not be ashamed of the testimony of our Lord, nor of me His prisoner, but share with me in the sufferings for the gospel according to the power of God,

Endurance Empowers

Exodus 18:23 (KJV): If thou shalt do this thing, and God command thee so, then thou shalt be able to endure, and all this people shall also go to their place in peace.

1 Thessalonians 1:3 (NIV): We remember before our God and Father your work produced by faith, your labor prompted by love, and your endurance inspired by hope in our Lord Jesus

Philippians 4:13 (NKJV): I can do all things through Christ who strengthens me.

<u>Protect the Innocence of Childhood</u>

> Psalm 71:17 (KJV): O God, You have taught me from my youth and to this day I declare Your wondrous works.

> Hebrews 12:8-9 (MSG): He's treating you as dear children. This trouble you're in isn't punishment; it's training, the normal experience of children. Only irresponsible parents leave children to fend for themselves. Would you prefer an irresponsible God?

> 3 John 1:4 (MSG): Nothing could make me happier than getting reports that my children continue diligently in the way of Truth!

<u>Be There</u>

> Exodus 16:7 (KJV): And in the morning, then ye shall see the glory of the Lord; for that he heareth your murmurings against the Lord: and what are we, that ye murmur against us?

> Acts 2:28 (KJV): Thou hast made known to me the ways of life; thou shalt make me full of joy with thy countenance.

<u>Bring Music to Life</u>

> Psalm 92:1 (KJV): It is a good thing to give thanks unto the Lord, and to sing praises unto thy name, O Most High.

Psalm 71:23 (CEB): My lips will rejoice aloud when I make music for you; my whole being, which you saved, will do the same.

Mentor Young Men and Women

Titus 2:4 (CEB): That way they can mentor young women to love their husbands and children,

1 Timothy 4:11 (CEB): Command these things. Teach them.

Romance Your Spouse

Hosea 2:19 (CEB): I will take you for my wife forever; I will take you for my wife in righteousness and in justice, in devoted love, and in mercy.

Ephesians 5:28 (CEB): That's how husbands ought to love their wives—in the same way as they do their own bodies. Anyone who loves his wife loves himself.

Honor Your Spouse

1 Peter 3:7 (CEB): Husbands, likewise, submit by living with your wife in ways that honor her, knowing that she is the weaker partner. Honor her all the more, as she is also a coheir of the gracious care of life. Do this so that your prayers won't be hindered.

Live Your Life

Psalm 23:6 (CEB): Yes, goodness and faithful love will pursue me all the days of my life, and I will live in the Lord's house as long as I live.

John 11:2 (CEB): Jesus said to her, "I am the resurrection and the life. Whoever believes in me will live, even though they die.

1 Corinthians 7:17 (CEB): Nevertheless, each person should live the kind of life that the Lord assigned when he called each one. This is what I teach in all the churches.

Glean from Greatness

Exodus 15:13 (CEB): With your great loyalty you led the people you rescued; with your power you guided them to your sanctuary.

Philippians 1:7 (CEB): I have good reason to think this way about all of you because I keep you in my heart. You are all my partners in God's grace, both during my time in prison and in the defense and support of the gospel.

Philemon 1:7 (CEB): I have great joy and encouragement because of your love, since the hearts of God's people are refreshed by your actions, my brother.

Work Willingly

Ecclesiastes 8:15 (CEB): So I commend enjoyment because there's nothing better for people to do under the sun but to eat, drink, and be glad. This is what will accompany them in their hard work, during the lifetime that God gives under the sun.

Pass on the Path of the Flesh

Genesis 6:3 (CEB): The Lord said, "My breath will not remain in humans forever, because they are flesh.

Psalm 78:39 (CEB): God kept remembering that they were just flesh, just breath that passes and doesn't come back.

Proverbs 5:11 (CEB): You will groan at the end when your body and flesh are exhausted,

1 Corinthians 15:50 (CEB): This is what I'm saying, brothers and sisters: Flesh and blood can't inherit the kingdom of heaven. Something that rots can't inherit something that doesn't decay.

Pursue the Path of the Spirit

Psalm 142:3 (CEB): When my spirit is weak inside me, you still know my way. But they've hidden a trap for me in the path I'm taking.

John 4:23 (CEB): But the time is coming—and is here!—when true worshippers will worship in spirit and truth. The Father looks for those who worship him this way.

Study the Scriptures

Ecclesiastes 12:12 (KJV): And further, my son, be admonished by these. Of making many books there is no end, and much study is wearisome to the flesh.

2 Timothy 2:15 (KJV): Study to shew thyself approved unto God, a workman that needeth not to be ashamed, rightly dividing the word of truth.

Grab the Gospel of Grace

Acts 20:24 (KJV): But none of these things move me, neither count I my life dear unto myself, so that I might finish my course with joy, and the ministry, which I have received of the Lord Jesus, to testify the gospel of the grace of God.

Galatians 1:6 (KJV): I marvel that ye are so soon removed from him that called you into the grace of Christ unto another gospel:

Philippians 1:7(KJV): Even as it is meet for me to think this of you all, because I have you in my heart; in as much as both in my bonds, and in the defense and confirmation of the gospel, ye all are partakers of my grace.

Play with Purpose

1 Kings 5:5 (KJV): And, behold, I purpose to build an house unto the name of the LORD my God, as the LORD spake unto David my father, saying, Thy son, whom I will set upon thy throne in thy room, he shall build an house unto my name.

Ecclesiastes 3:1 (KJV): To every thing there is a season, and a time to every purpose under the heaven:

Romans 8:28 And we know that all things work together for good to them that love God, to them who are the called according to his purpose.

Find Truth in Scripture

Daniel 10:2 (KJV): But I will show thee that which is noted in the scripture of truth:

Psalm 138:2 (KJV): I will worship toward thy holy temple, and praise thy name for thy lovingkindness and for thy truth: for thou hast magnified thy word above all thy name.

Ephesians 1:13 (KJV): In whom ye also trusted, after that ye heard the word of truth, the gospel of your salvation: in whom also after that ye believed, ye were sealed with that holy Spirit of promise,

Colossians 1:5 (KJV): For the hope which is laid up for you in heaven, whereof ye heard before in the word of the truth of the gospel;

Learn the Gospel of Grace

2 Corinthians 8:7 (KJV): Therefore, as ye abound in everything, in faith, and utterance, and knowledge, and in all diligence, and in your love to us, see that ye abound in this grace also.

2 Peter 1:2 (KJV): Grace and peace be multiplied unto you through the knowledge of God, and of Jesus our Lord.

2 Peter 3:18 (KJV): But grow in grace, and in the knowledge of our Lord and Saviour Jesus Christ. To him be glory both now and forever. Amen.

He Stands at Your Door

John 10:1 (KJV): Verily, verily, I say unto you, He that entereth not by the door into the sheepfold, but climbeth up some other way, the same is a thief and a robber.

Revelation 3:20 (KJV): Behold, I stand at the door, and knock: if any man hear my voice, and open the door, I will come in to him, and will sup with him, and he with me.

Receive Christ Personally

Romans 5:17 (KJV): For if by one man's offence death reigned by one; much more they which receive abundance of grace and of the gift of righteousness shall reign in life by one, Jesus Christ.

Romans 15:7 (KJV): Wherefore receive ye one another, as Christ also received us to the glory of God.

Galatians 3:14 (KJV): That the blessing of Abraham might come on the Gentiles through Jesus Christ; that we might receive the promise of the Spirit through faith.

Colossians 3:24 (KJV): Knowing that of the Lord ye shall receive the reward of the inheritance: for ye serve the Lord Christ.

<u>Play Physical Games</u>

Psalm 35:9-10 (MSG): But let me run loose and free, celebrating GOD's great work, Every bone in my body laughing, singing, "GOD, there's no one like you. You put the down-and-out on their feet and protect the unprotected from bullies!"

1 Timothy 4:7-8 (MSG): Exercise daily in God—no spiritual flabbiness, please! Workouts in the gymnasium are useful, but a disciplined life in God is far more so, making you fit both today and forever

<u>Personal Faith in Christ</u>

Galatians 2:15 (MSG): We Jews know that we have no advantage of birth over "non-Jewish sinners." We know very well that we are not set right with God by rule-keeping but only through personal faith in Jesus Christ.

Galatians 2:20(MSG): The life you see me living is not "mine," but it is lived by faith in the Son of God, who loved me and gave himself for me. I am not going to go back on that. Is it not clear to you that to go back to that old rule-keeping, peer-pleasing religion would be an abandonment of everything personal and free in my relationship with God? I refuse to do that, to repudiate God's grace

Romans 5:1 (KJV): Therefore being justified by faith, we have peace with God through our Lord Jesus Christ:

Live Your Faith

Psalm 61:6-8 (MSG): Let the days of the king add up to years and years of good rule. Set his throne in the full light of God; post Steady Love and Good Faith as lookouts, And I'll be the poet who sings your glory— and live what I sing every day.

2 Corinthians 1:24 (MSG): We're not in charge of how you live out the faith, looking over your shoulders, suspiciously critical. We're partners, working alongside you, joyfully expectant. I know that you stand by your own faith, not by ours.

Galatians 2:1(KJV): Knowing that a man is not justified by the works of the law, but by the faith of Jesus Christ, even we have believed in Jesus Christ, that we might be justified by the faith of Christ, and not by the works of the law: for by the works of the law shall no flesh be justified.

Dance in Delight

Jeremiah 31:13 (MSG): Young women will dance and be happy, young men and old men will join in. I'll convert their weeping into laughter, lavishing comfort, invading their grief with joy.

Proverbs 23:15-16 (MSG): Dear child, if you become wise, I'll be one happy parent. My heart will dance and sing to the tuneful truth you'll speak.

1 Corinthians 10:6 (MSG): The same thing could happen to us. We must be on guard so that we never get caught up in wanting our own way as they did. And we must

not turn our religion into a circus as they did—"First the people partied, then they threw a dance."

Pursue Righteousness

Isaiah 51:1 (NIV): "Listen to me, you who pursue righteousness and who seek the LORD: Look to the rock from which you were cut and to the quarry from which you were hewn;

Matthew 6:33 (NIV): But seek first his kingdom and his righteousness, and all these things will be given to you as well.

Continue Your Course

Psalm 119:1(MSG): You're blessed when you stay on course, walking steadily on the road revealed by God. You're blessed when you follow his directions, doing your best to find him. That's right—you don't go off on your own; you walk straight along the road he set. You, God, prescribed the right way to live now you expect us to live it. Oh, that my steps might be steady, keeping to the course you set;

1 Corinthians 10:13 (MSG): No test or temptation that comes your way is beyond the course of what others have had to face. All you need to remember is that God will never let you down; he'll never let you be pushed past your limit; he'll always be there to help you come through it.

Selfishness Sinks

Romans 8:4-5 (CEB): He did this so that the righteous requirement of the Law might be fulfilled in us. Now the way we live is based on the Spirit, not based on selfishness. People whose lives are based on selfishness think about selfish things, but people whose lives are based on the Spirit think about things that are related to the Spirit.

Galatians 5:16(CEB): (Two different ways of living) I say be guided by the Spirit and you won't carry out your selfish desires.

Philippians 2:3 (CEB): Don't do anything for selfish purposes, but with humility think of others as better than yourselves.

Fear Burns Out Your Fire

Genesis 26:24 (KJV): And the LORD appeared unto him the same night, and said, I am the God of Abraham thy father: fear not, for I am with thee, and will bless thee, and multiply thy seed for my servant Abraham's sake.

Deuteronomy 31:6 (KJV): Be strong and of a good courage, fear not, nor be afraid of them: for the LORD thy God, he it is that doth go with thee; he will not fail thee, nor forsake thee.

2 Timothy 1:7 (KJV): God hath not given us the spirit of fear; but of power, and of love, and of a sound mind.

<u>Read to Reach</u>

> Exodus 24:7 (MSG): Exodus 24:7 Then he took the Book of the Covenant and read it as the people listened

> Nehemiah 8:18 (MSG): Ezra read from the Book of The Revelation of God each day, from the first to the last day—they celebrated the feast for seven days. On the eighth day they held a solemn assembly in accordance with the decree.

> Romans 14:10-12 (MSG): So where does that leave you when you criticize a brother? And where does that leave you when you condescend to a sister? I'd say it leaves you looking pretty silly—or worse. Eventually, we're all going to end up kneeling side by side in the place of judgment, facing God. Your critical and condescending ways aren't going to improve your position there one bit. Read it for yourself in Scripture: "As I live and breathe," God says, "every knee will bow before me; Every tongue will tell the honest truth that I and only I am God." So tend to your knitting. You've got your hands full just taking care of your own life before God.

<u>No Dream, No Destiny</u>

> Lamentations 1:9 (NKJV): Her uncleanness is in her skirts; She did not consider her destiny; Therefore her collapse was awesome; She had no comforter. "O LORD, behold my affliction, For the enemy is exalted!"

Psalm 16:9-10 (MSG): I'm happy from the inside out, and from the outside in, I'm firmly formed. You canceled my ticket to hell— that's not my destination!

Galatians 3:25-27 (MSG): But now you have arrived at your destination: By faith in Christ you are in direct relationship with God.

Be a Team Member

2 Corinthians 9:5 (MSG): I've recruited these brothers as an advance team to get you and your promised offering all ready before I get there. I want you to have all the time you need to make this offering in your own way. I don't want anything forced or hurried at the last minute.

Acts 1:13 (MSG):They agreed they were in this for good, completely together in prayer, the women included. Also Jesus' mother, Mary, and his brothers.

1 John 3:14 (KJV): We know that we have passed from death unto life, because we love the brethren. He that loveth not his brother abideth in death.

Be Single-hearted for Christ

2 Samuel 17:10 (KJV): And he also that is valiant, whose heart is as the heart of a lion, shall utterly melt: for all Israel knoweth that thy father is a mighty man, and they which be with him are valiant men.

1 Chronicles 12:38 (KJV): All these men of war, that could keep rank, came with a perfect heart to Hebron, to

make David king over all Israel: and all the rest also of Israel were of one heart to make David king.

Hebrews 4:12 (KJV): For the word of God is alive and active. Sharper than any double-edged sword, it penetrates even to dividing soul and spirit, joints and marrow; it judges the thoughts and attitudes of the heart.

James 4:8 (KJV): Come near to God and he will come near to you. Wash your hands, you sinners, and purify your hearts, you double-minded.

Walk Your Talk

Psalm 115:3-8 (MSG): Our God is in heaven doing whatever he wants to do. Their gods are metal and wood, handmade in a basement shop: Carved mouths that can't talk, painted eyes that can't see, Tin ears that can't hear, molded noses that can't smell, Hands that can't grasp, feet that can't walk or run, throats that never utter a sound. Those who make them have become just like them, have become just like the gods they trust.

James 2:16-17 (MSG): Be clothed in Christ! Be filled with the Holy Spirit!" and walk off without providing so much as a coat or a cup of soup—where does that get you? Isn't it obvious that God-talk without God-acts is outrageous nonsense?